I0467347

COLOR
Babylonian Art

Conceived, Designed, and Illustrated by:

Mrinal Mitra

Series Edited by:

Swarna Mitra & **Malika Mitra**

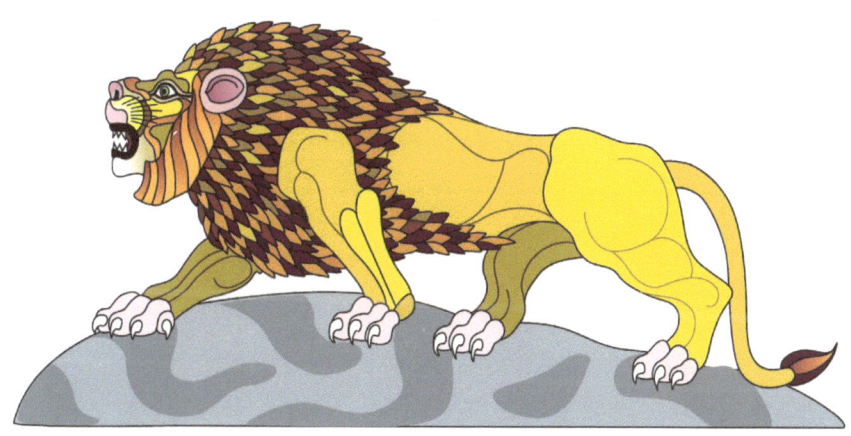

WORLD CULTURE COLORING SERIES

This series is dedicated to the citizens of the world;
from the young blooming minds of children, to the aspired individuals of all ages.

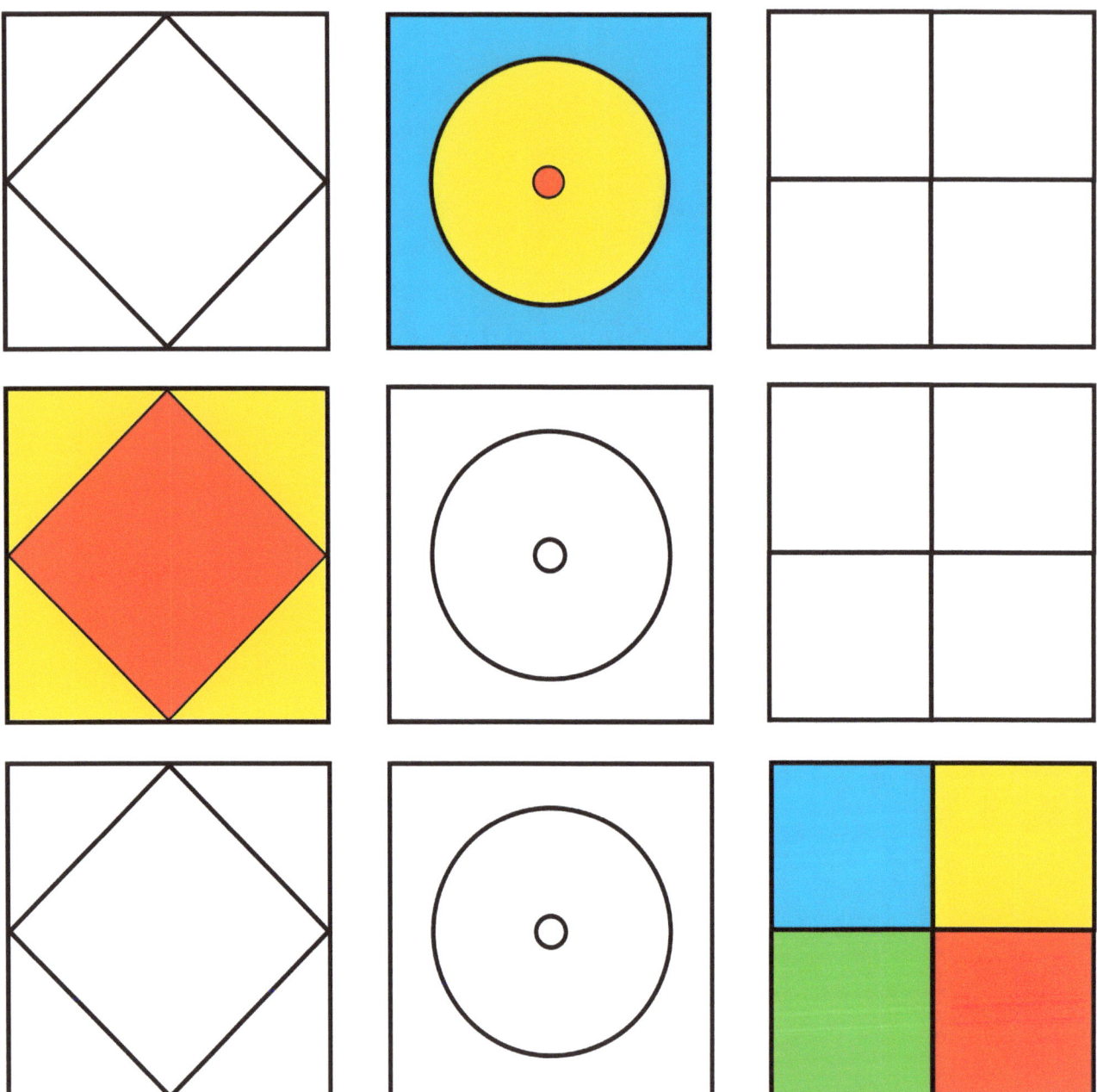

*Facing pages: The ancient Babylonian Geometrical Tablets were used
to calculate the area of subdivisions of a square in the1800 B.C.E.*

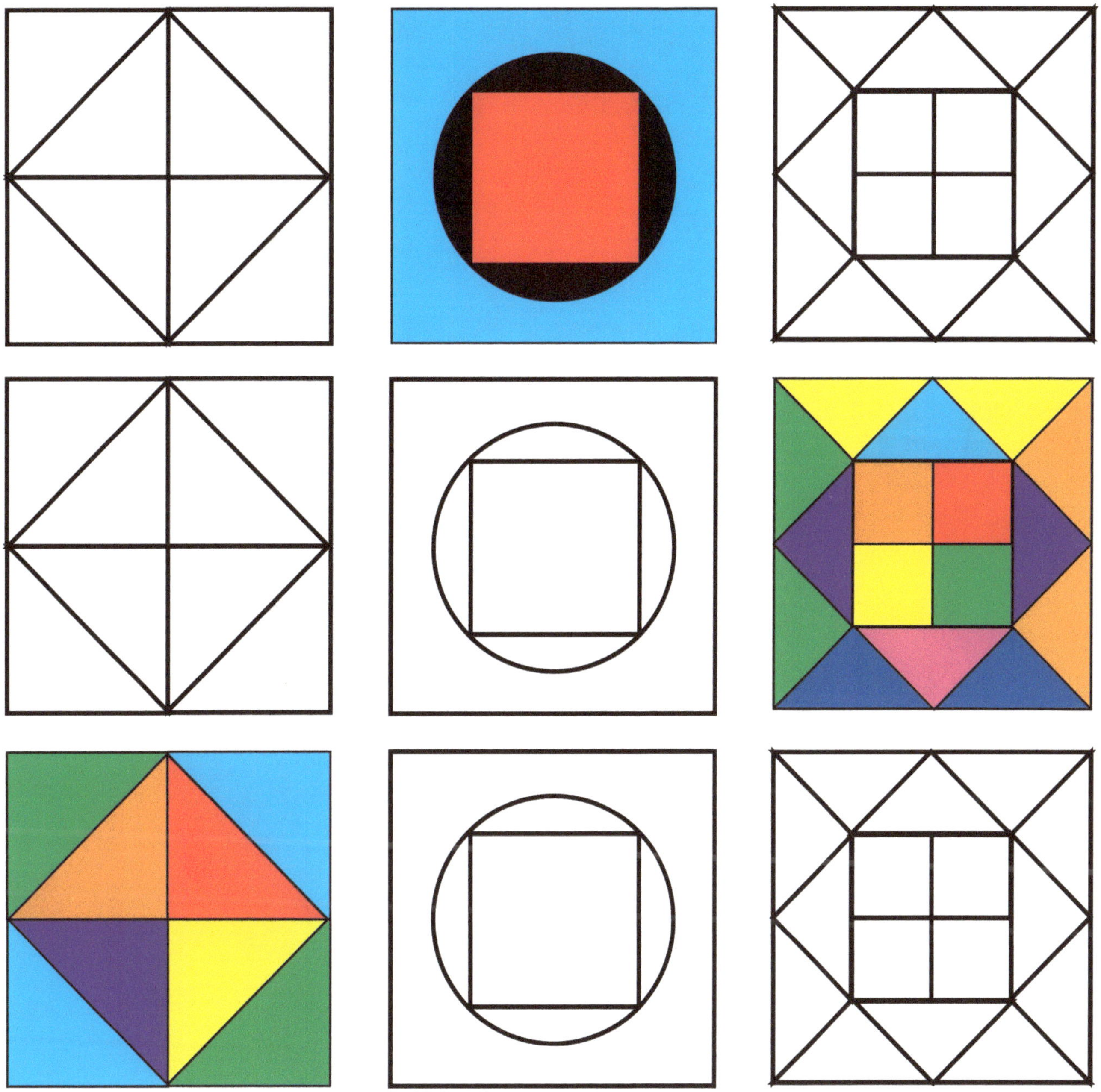

Color the drawings above using your preferred choice of colors.

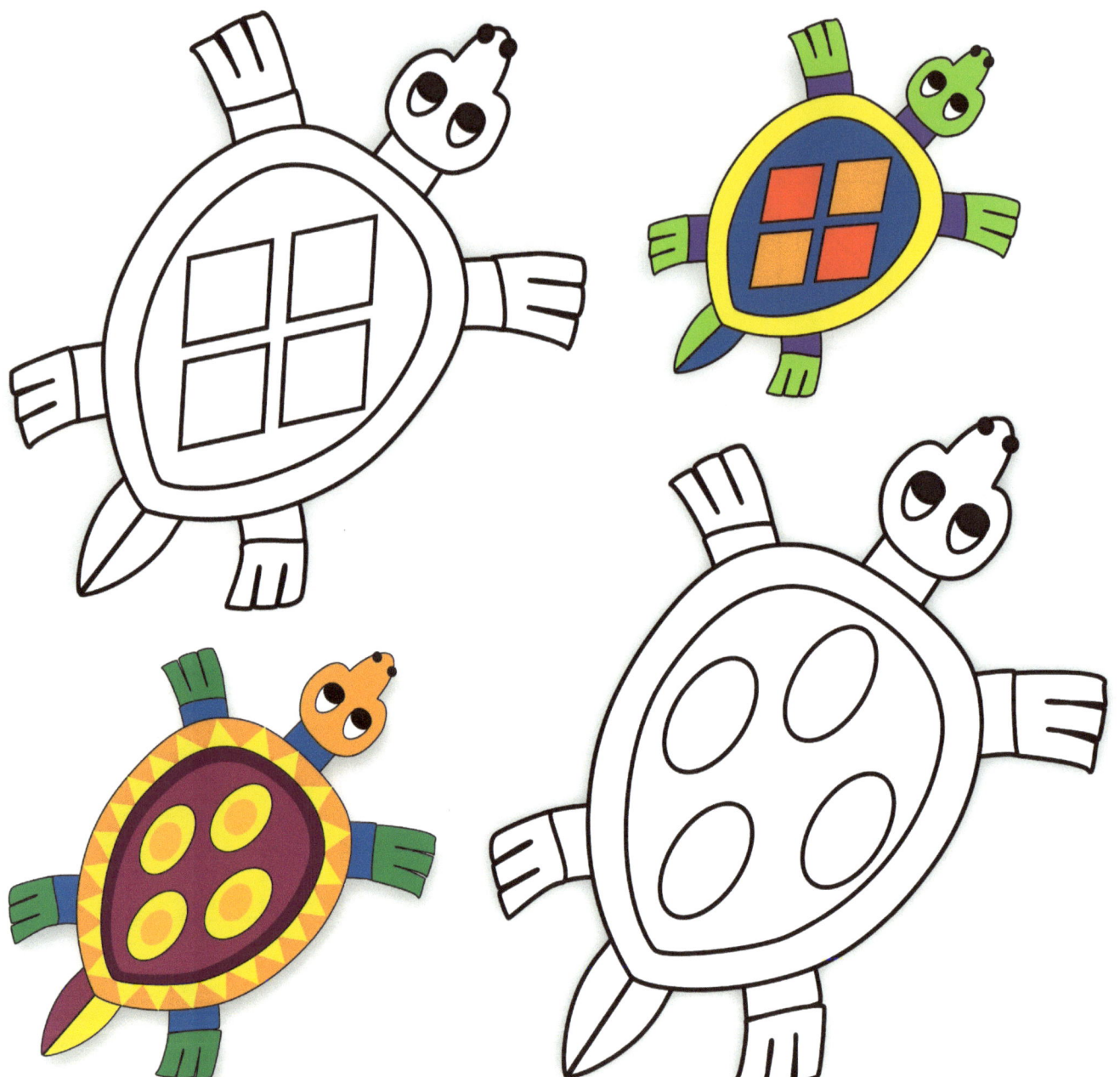

Facing pages: Turtles as symbol of God on stone. Kassites, Babylonia. 1120 B.C.E.

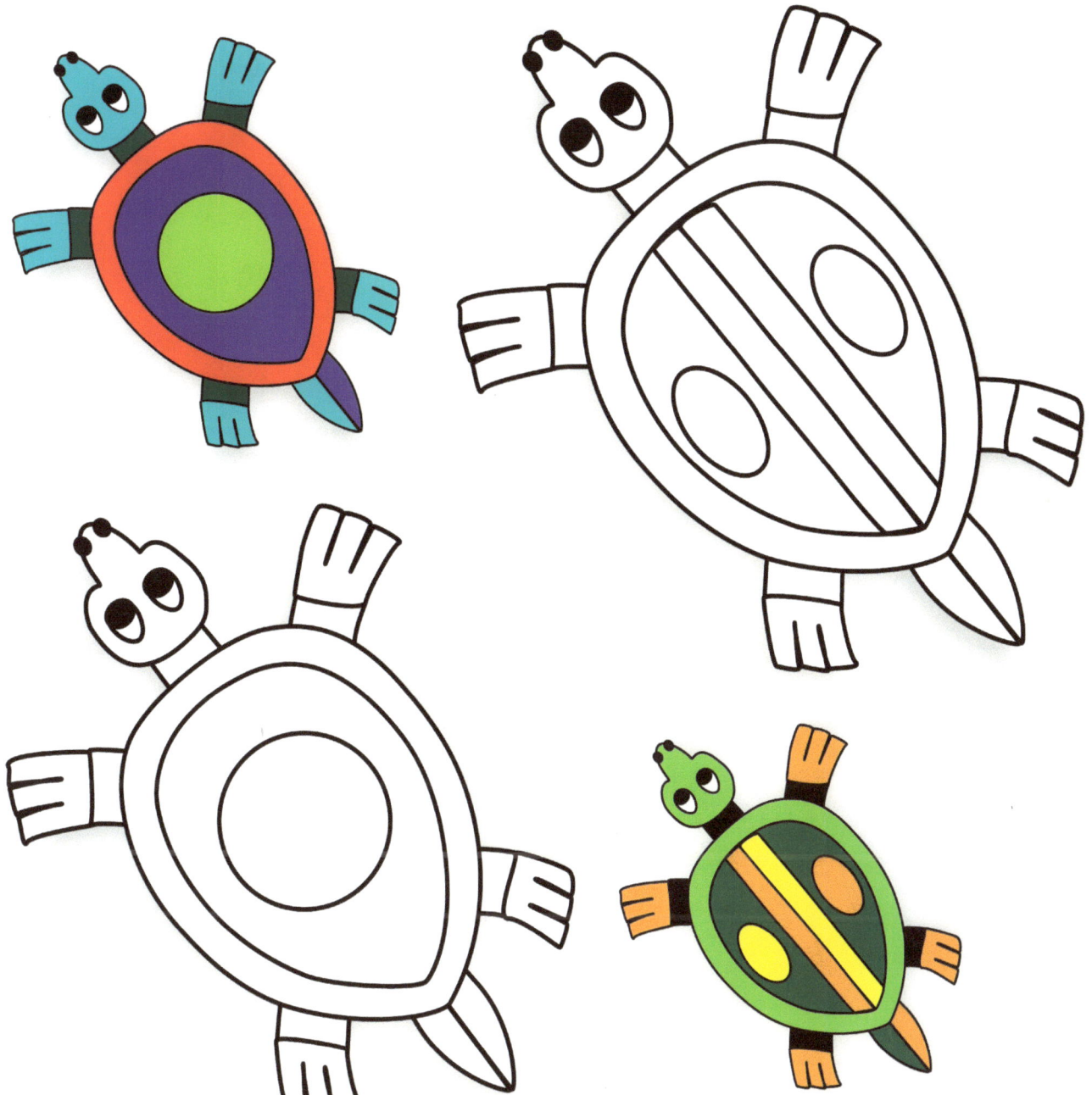

Color the drawings above using your preferred choice of colors.

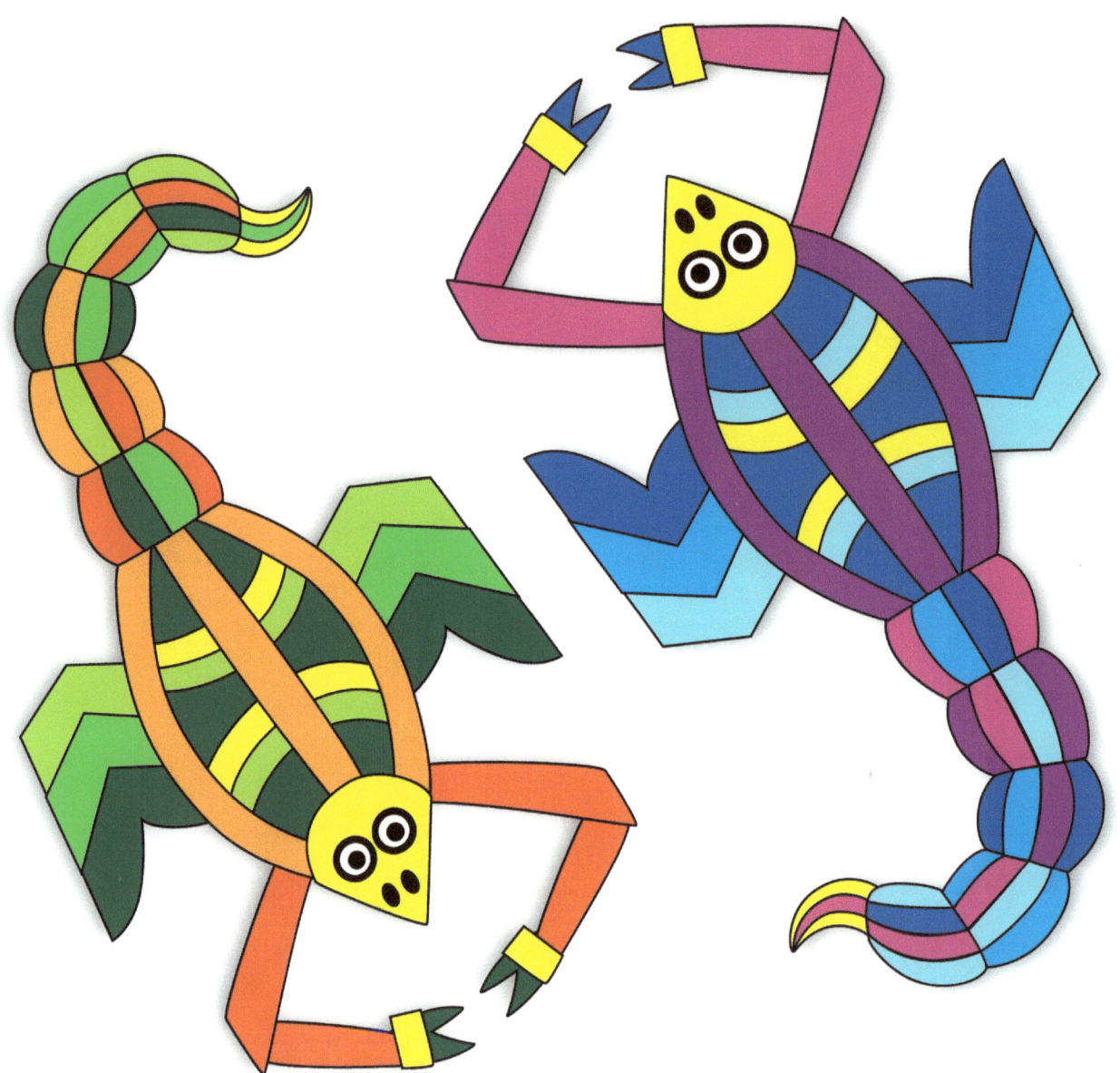

Scorpion as symbol of God invoked on a boundary stone, a type
introduced by the Kassites, during Babylonian Civilization. 12th Century B.C.E.

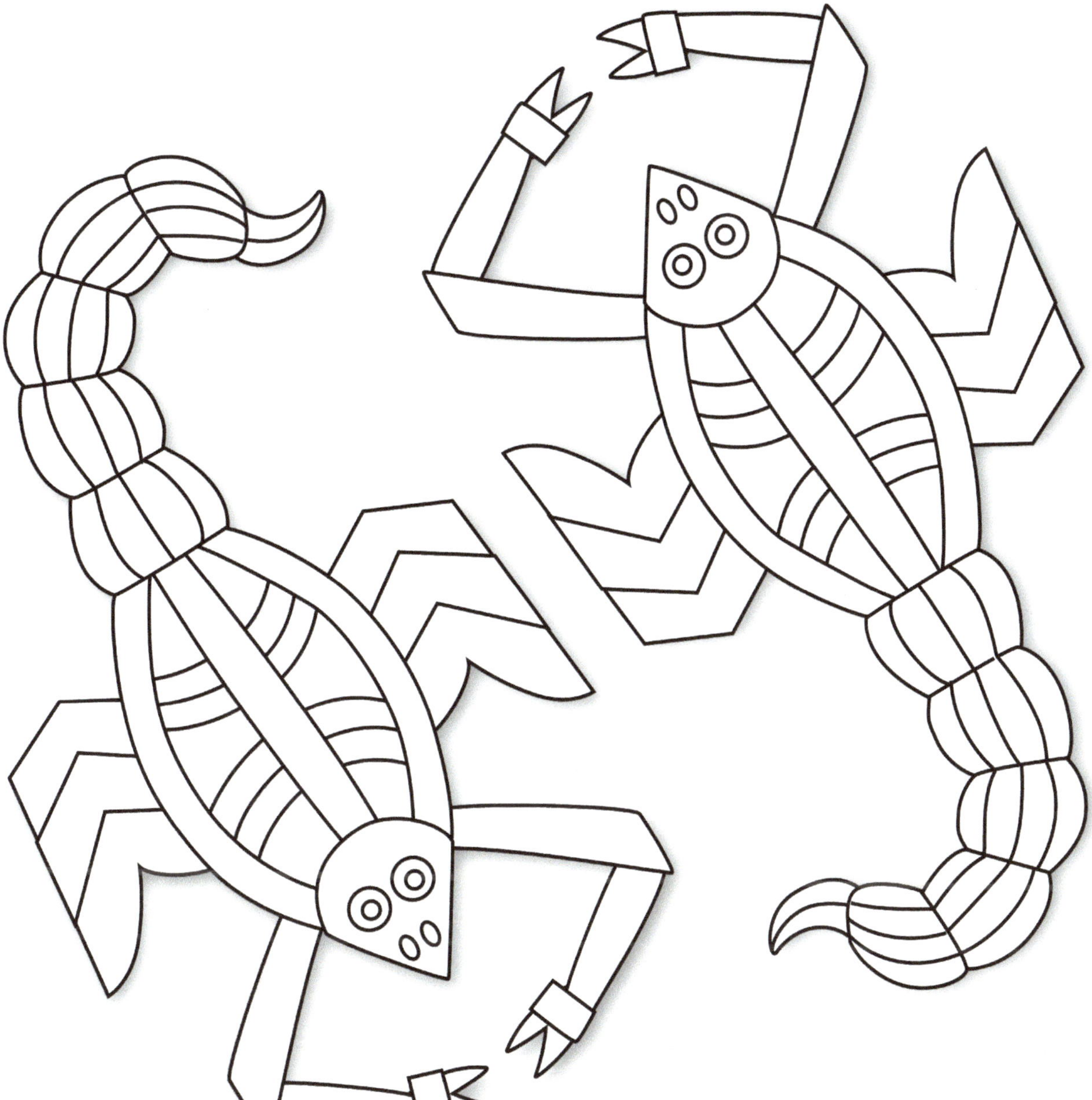

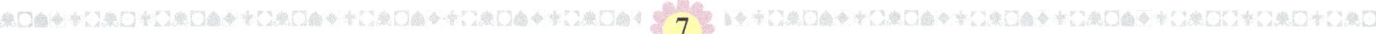

Color the drawings above using your preferred choice of colors.

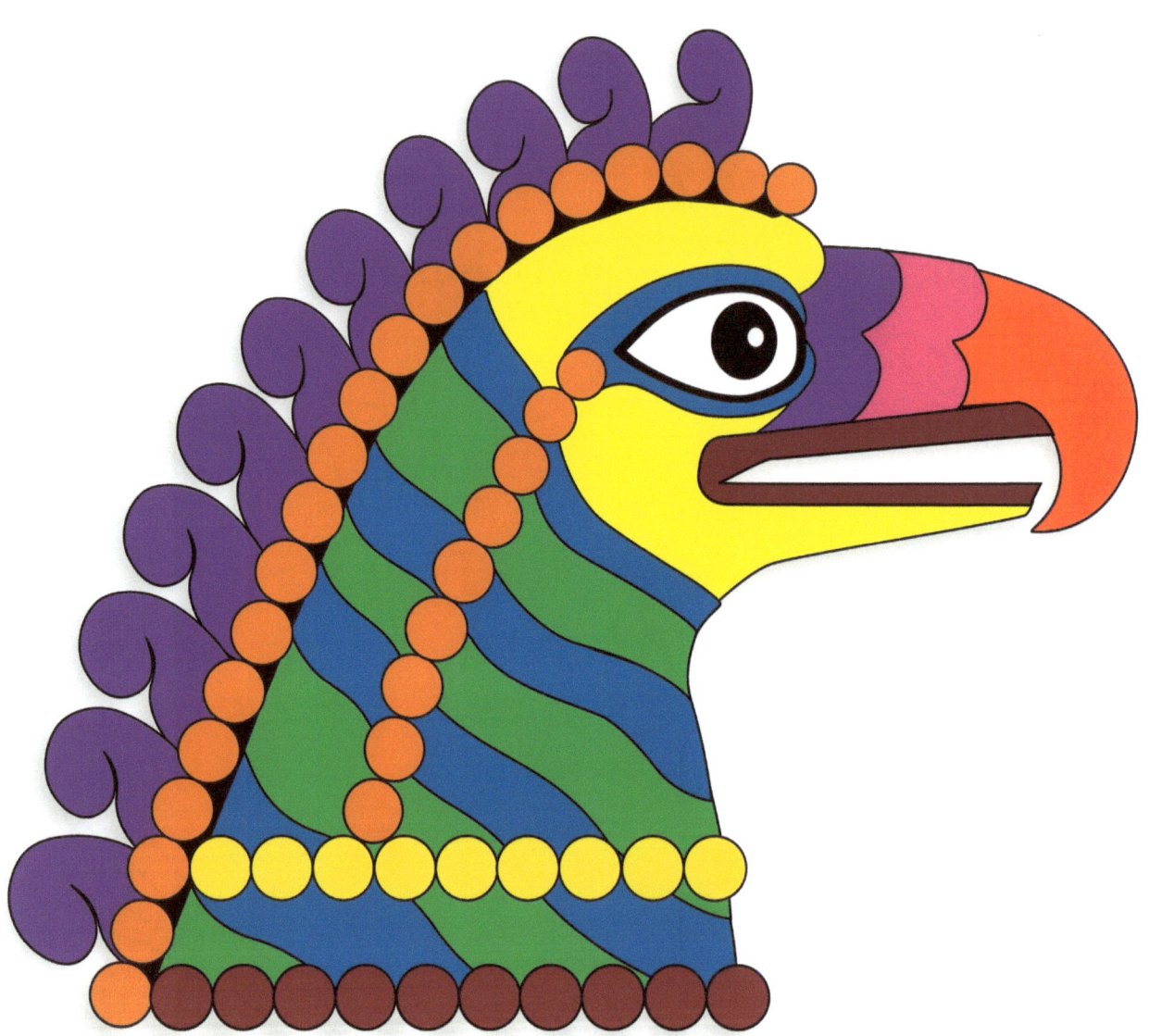

An eagle head of a genie. Relief work in an inner room lined with ritual scenes.
Ashurnasirpal ceremonial room decoration.

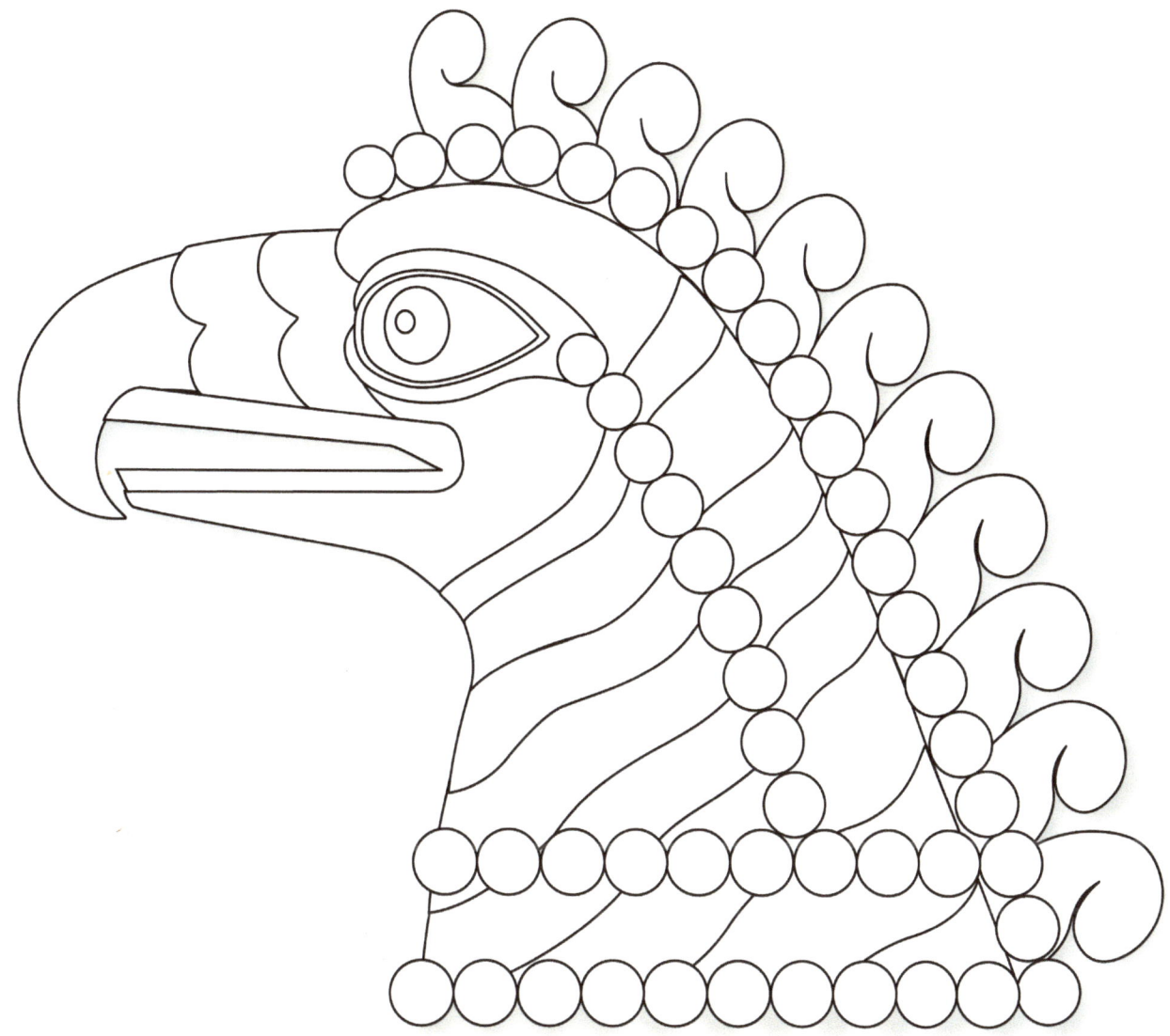

Color the drawing above using your preferred choice of colors.

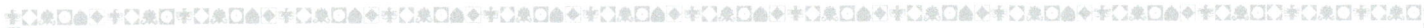

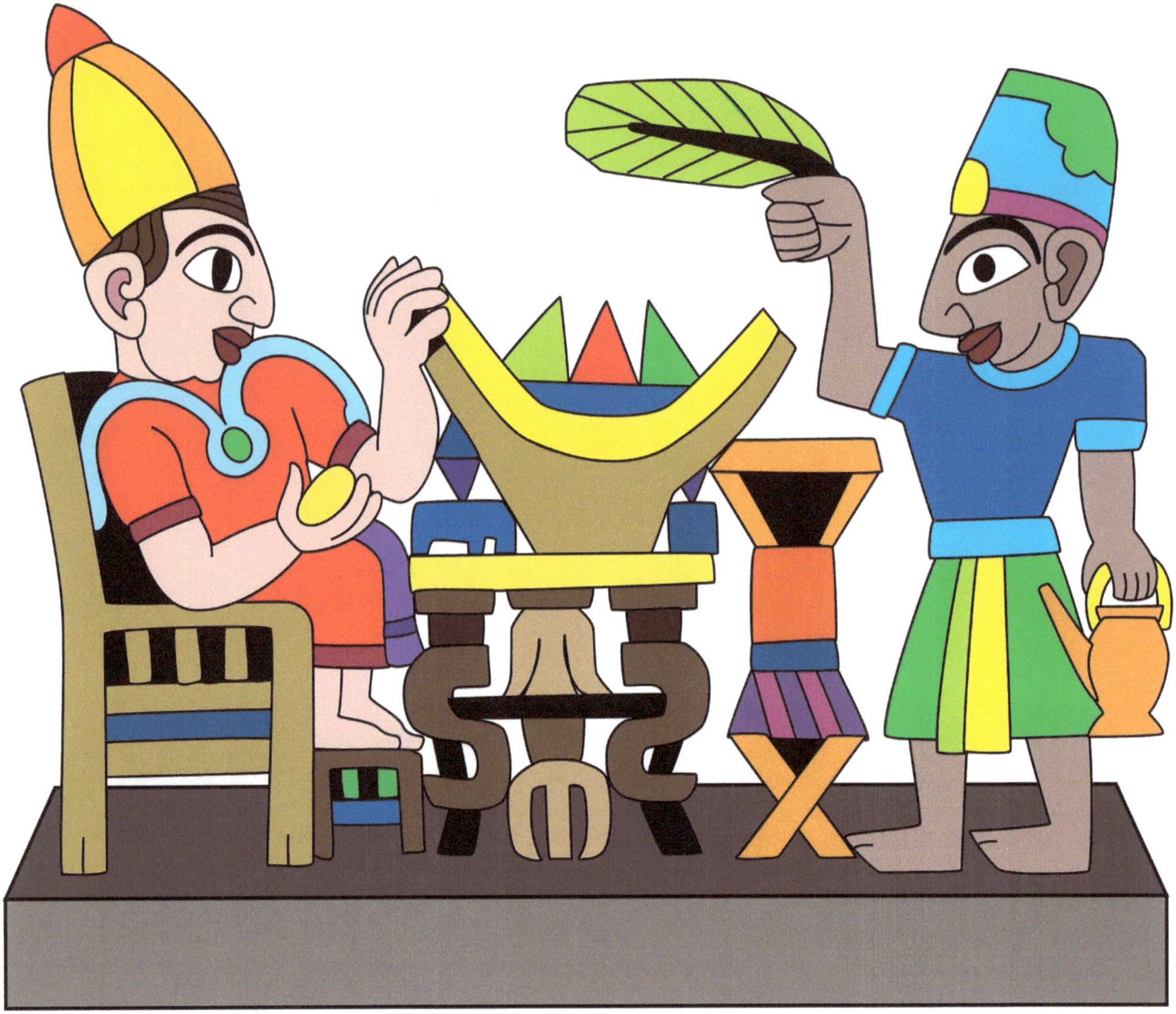

Part of a Neo-Hittite relief from the palace of Sanduarri in Karatepe, Cilicia. The king is banqueting with the musicians. A coarse imitation of Assyrian scenes. 7th Century B.C.E.

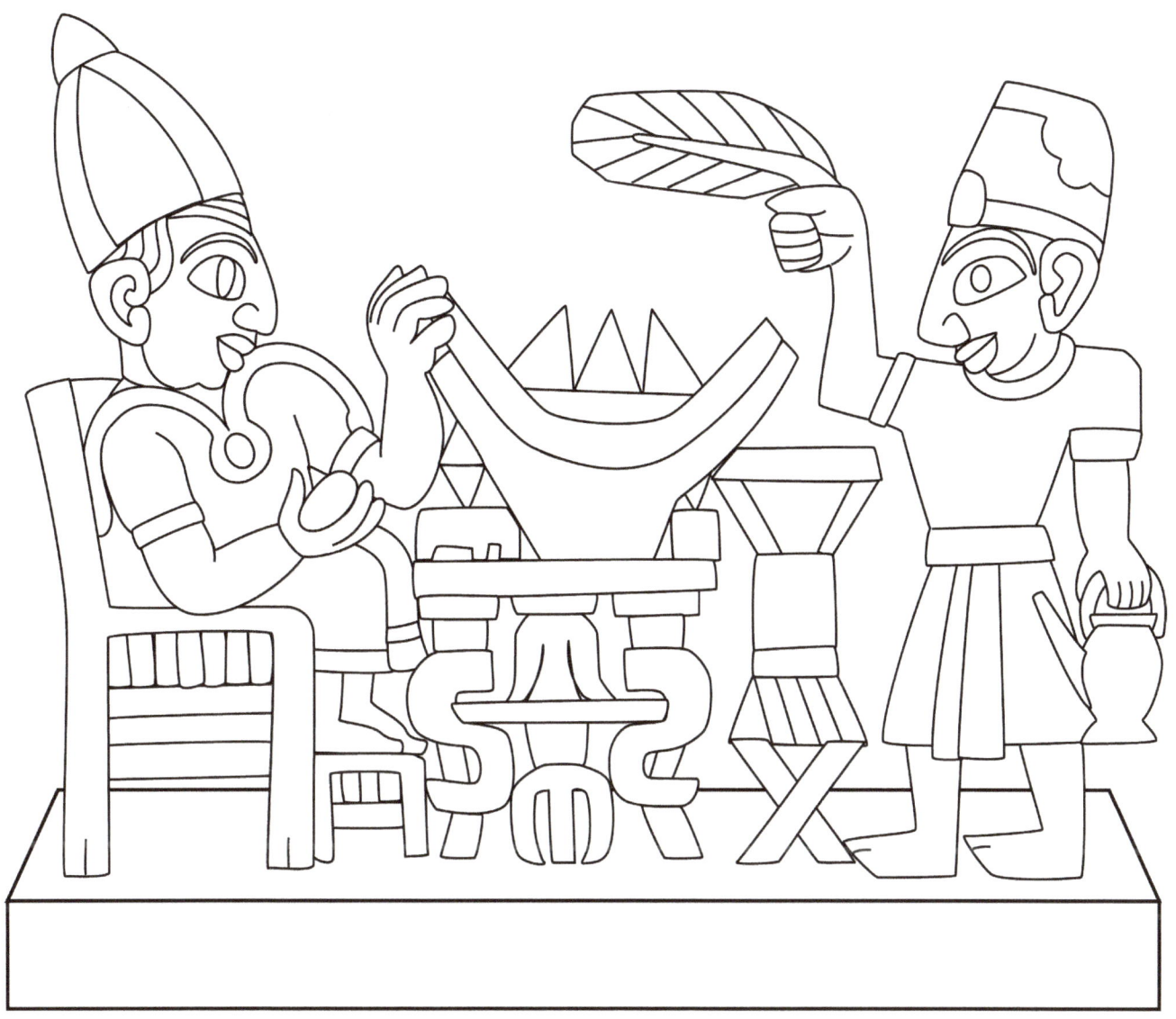

Color the drawing above using your preferred choice of colors.

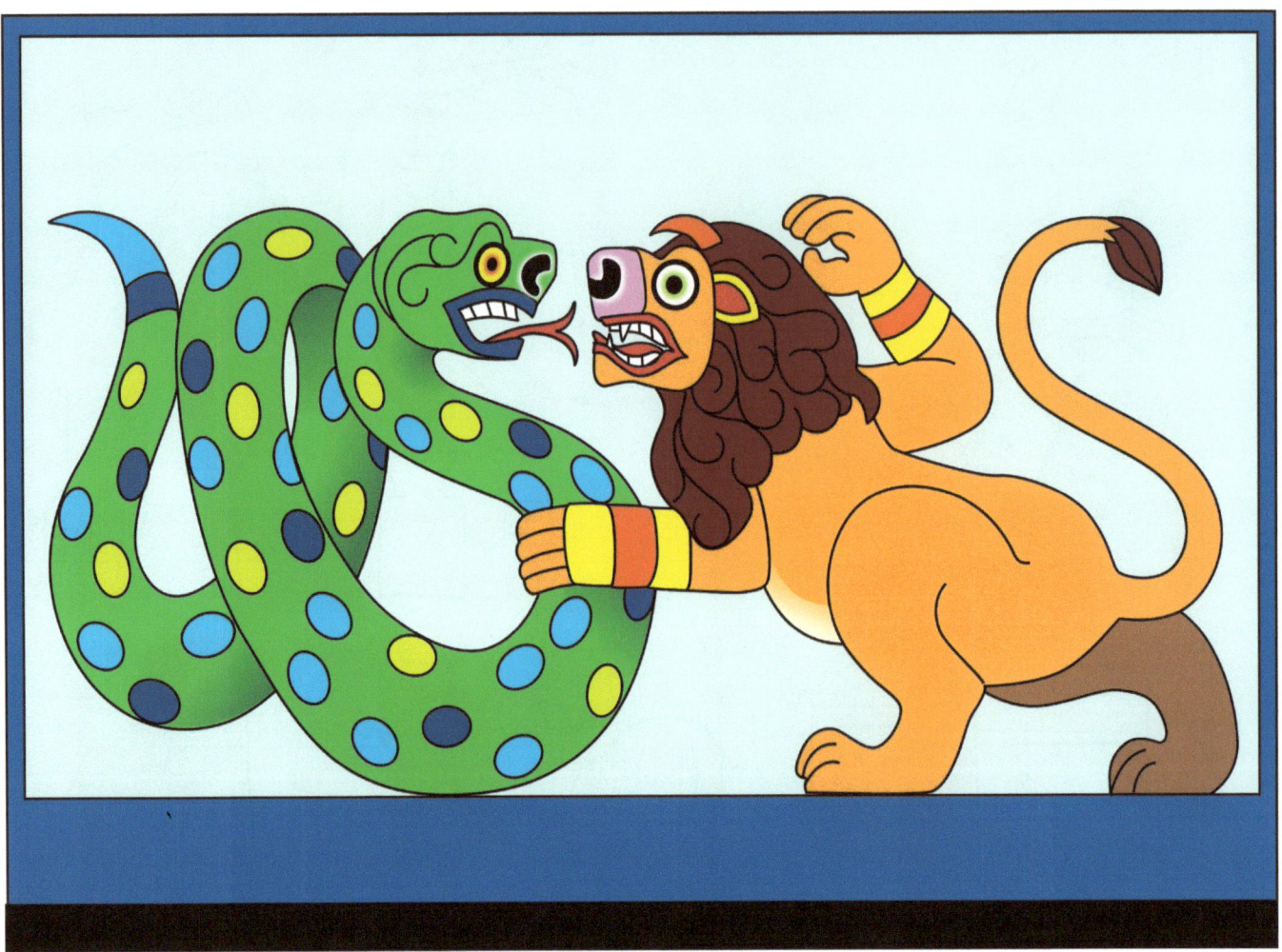

A combat between the King of Snakes and the King of Beasts.
On a stone bowl from Inanna Temple, Baghdad. 11th Century, B.C.E.

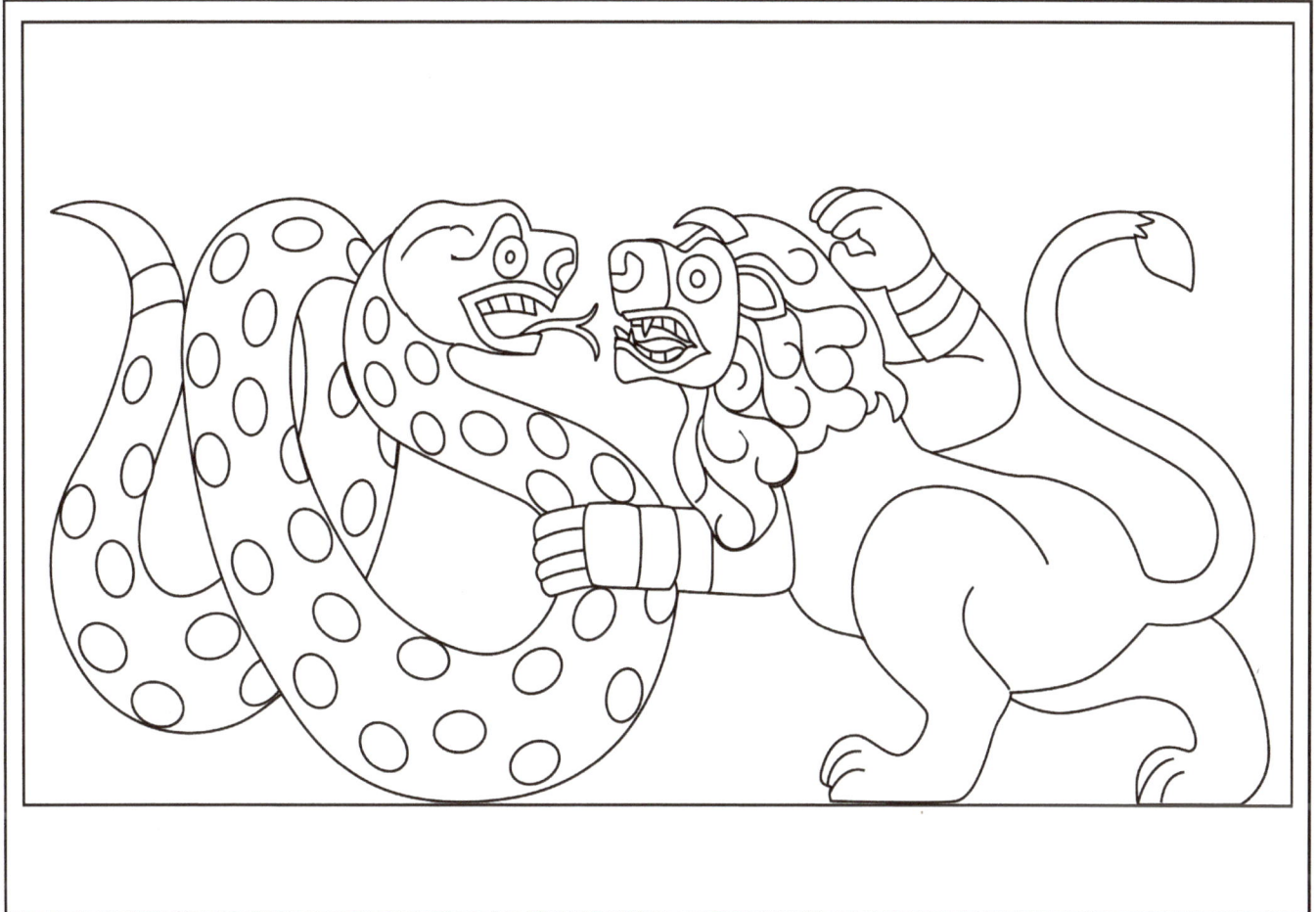

Color the drawing above using your preferred choice of colors.

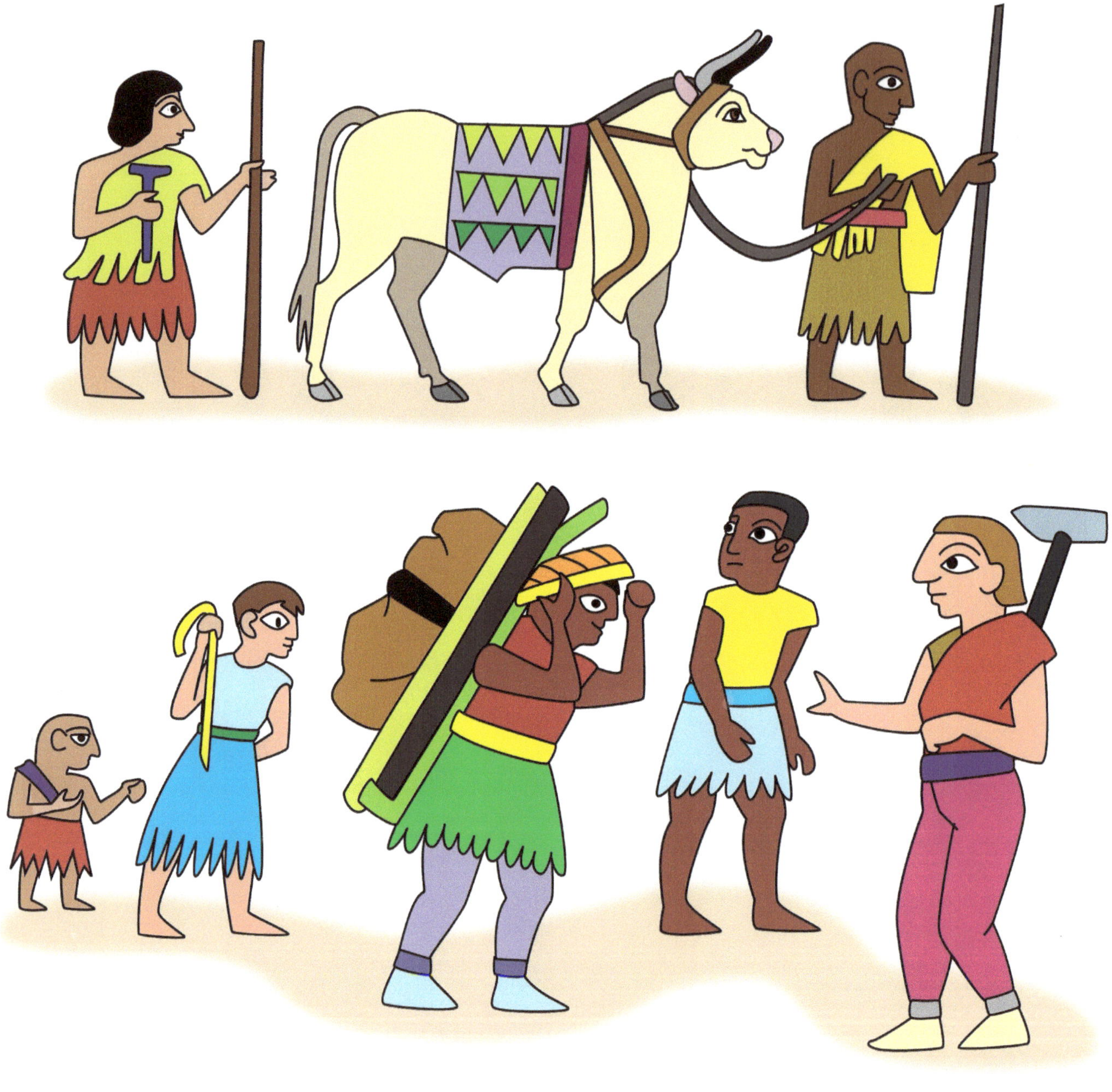

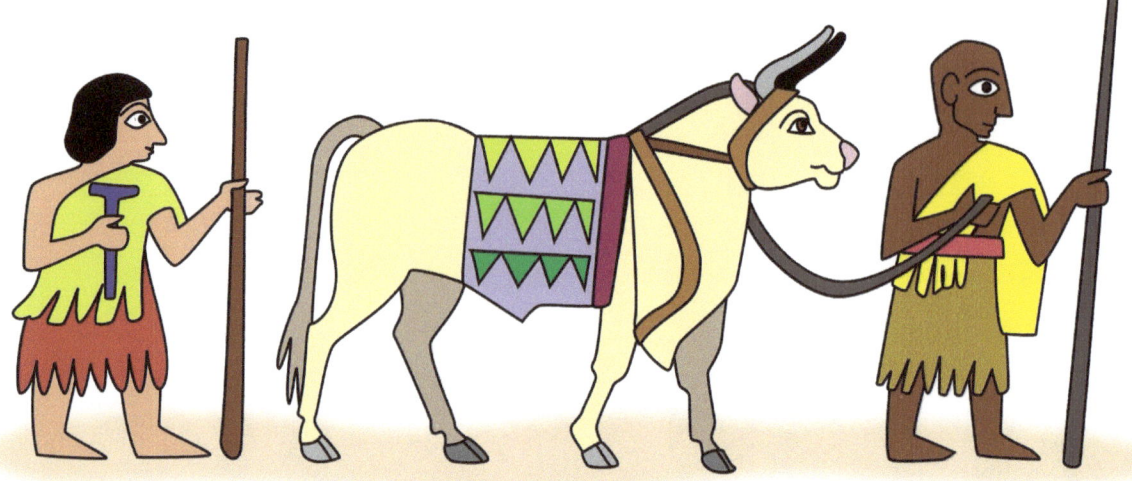

A victory celebration scene in Grave 779, when Ur (Urim) held the "Kingship of Sumerian."

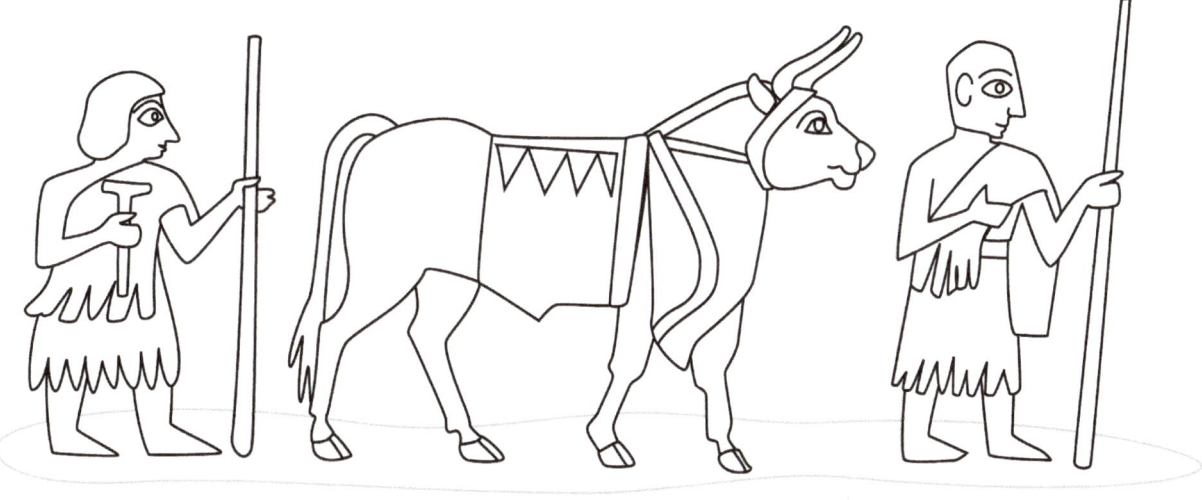

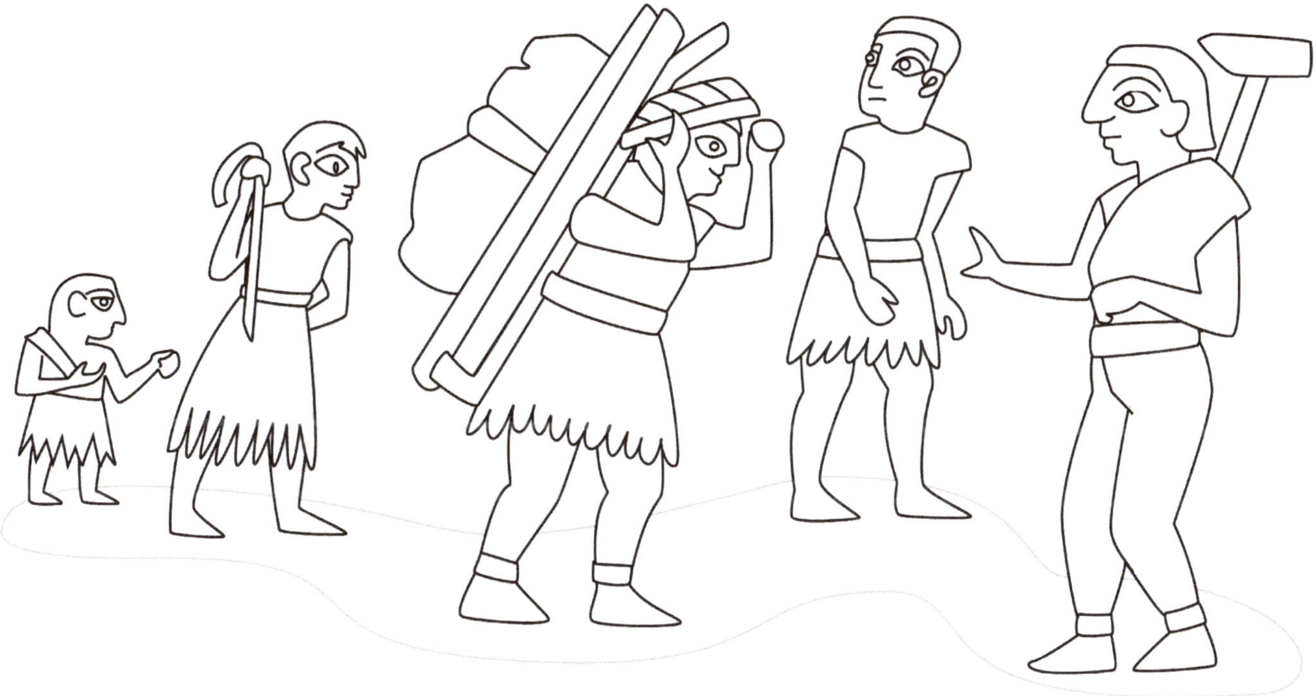

Color the drawings above using your preferred choice of colors.

15

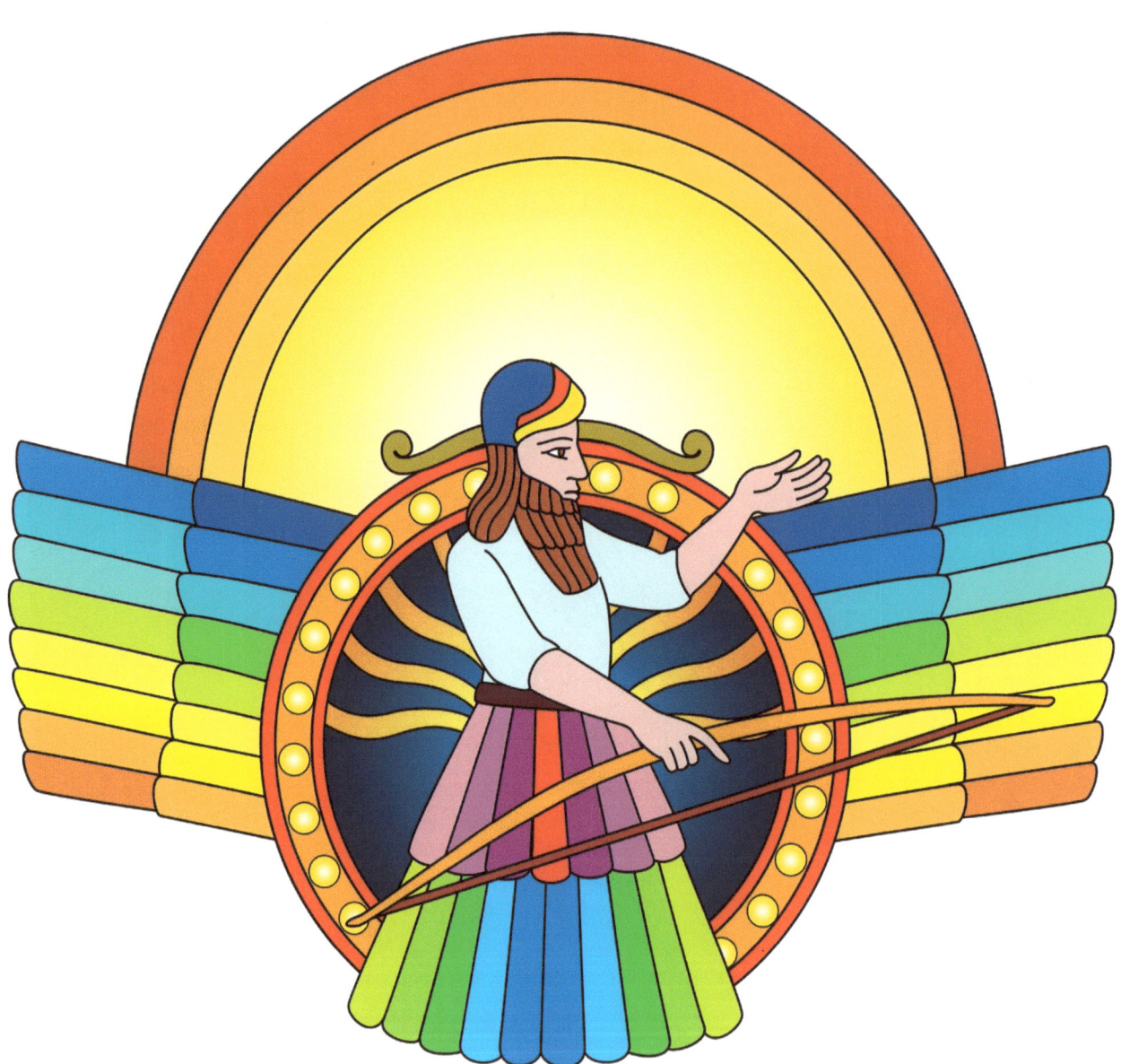

Assur, the Assyrian god on a sun-disk, 5th Century B.C.E.

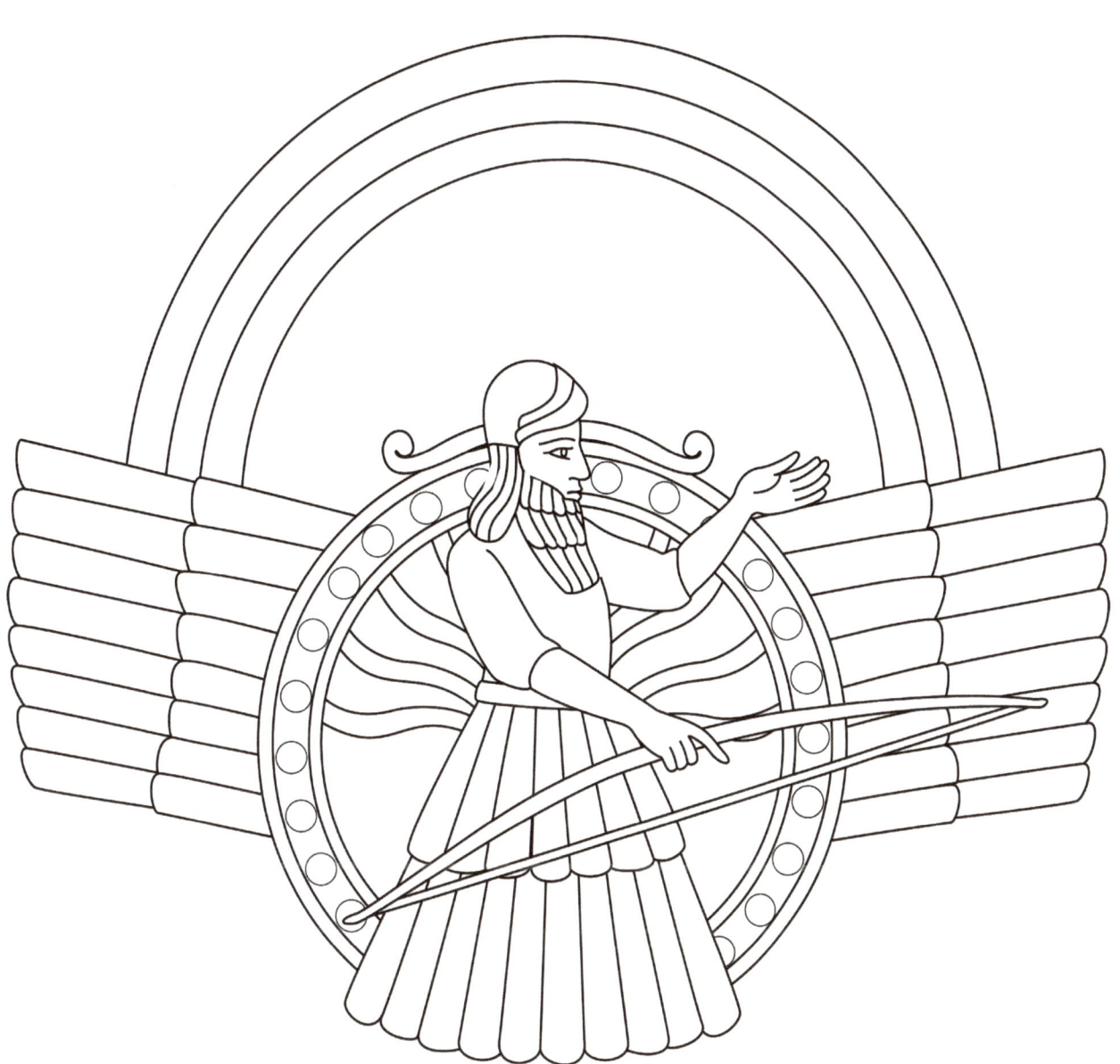

Color the drawing above using your preferred choice of colors.

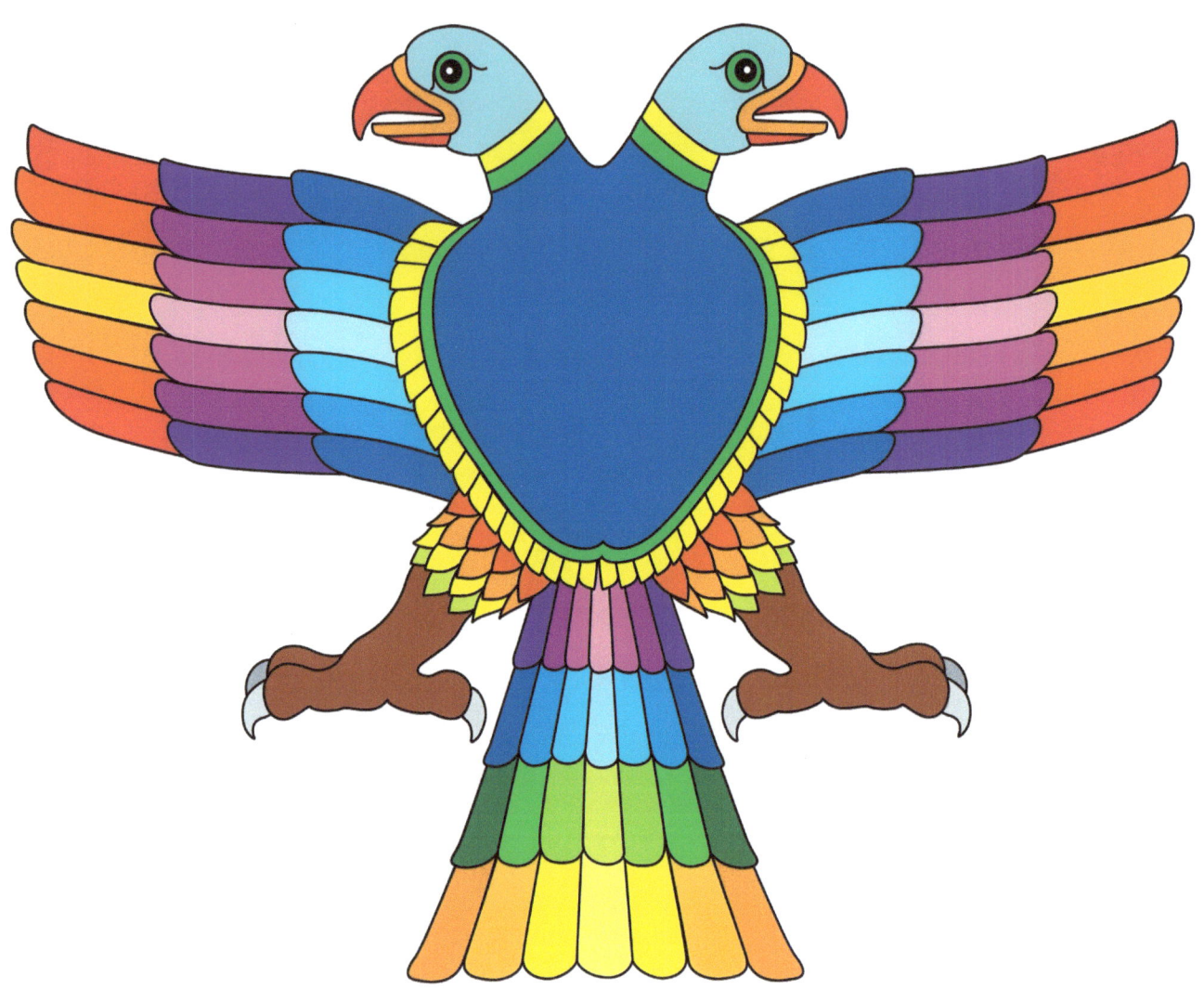

Double-headed eagle gripping two hares (not shown).
Relief work from the Sphinx Gate at Alaca Huyuk, 14th Century B.C.E.

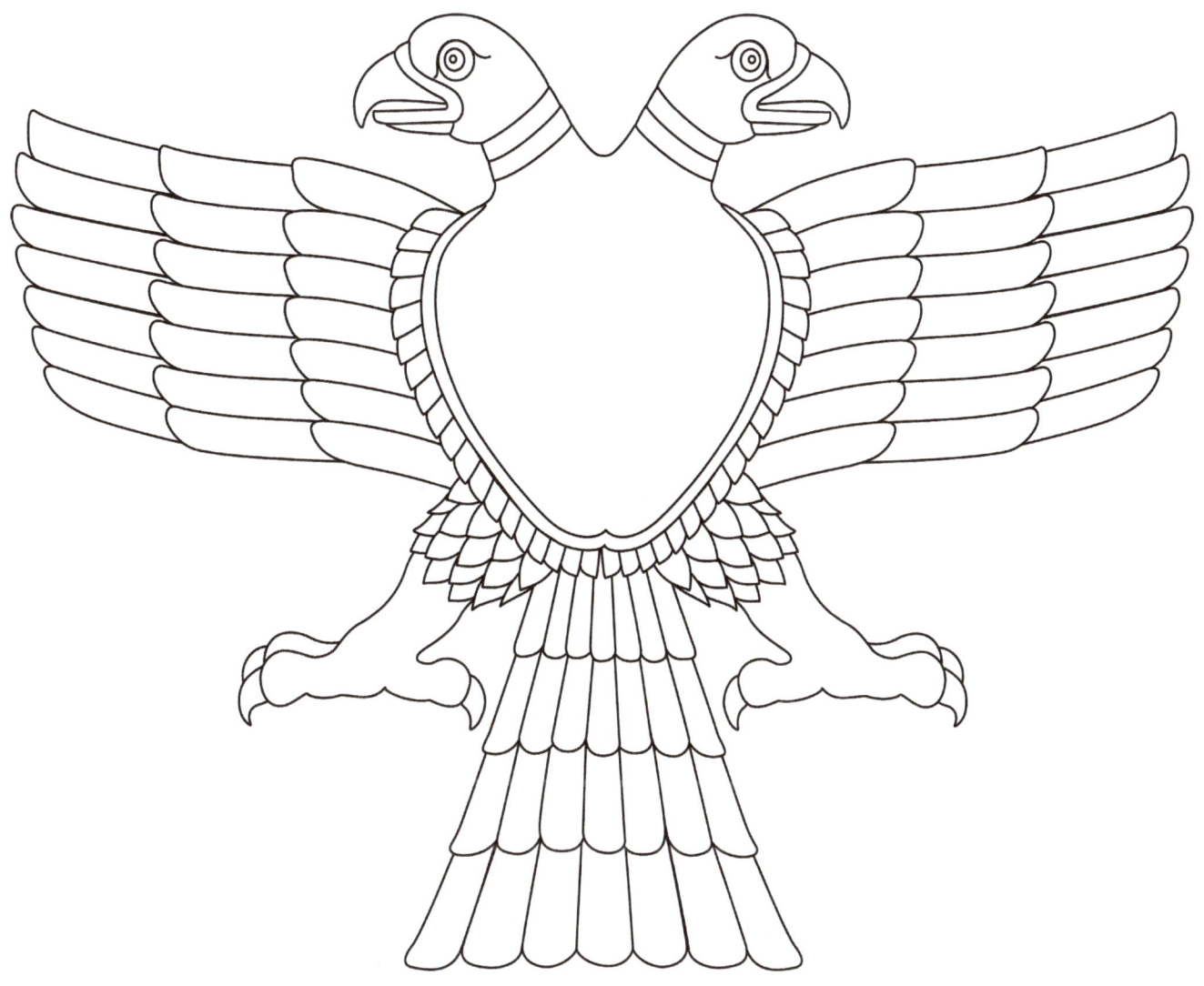

Color the drawing above using your preferred choice of colors.

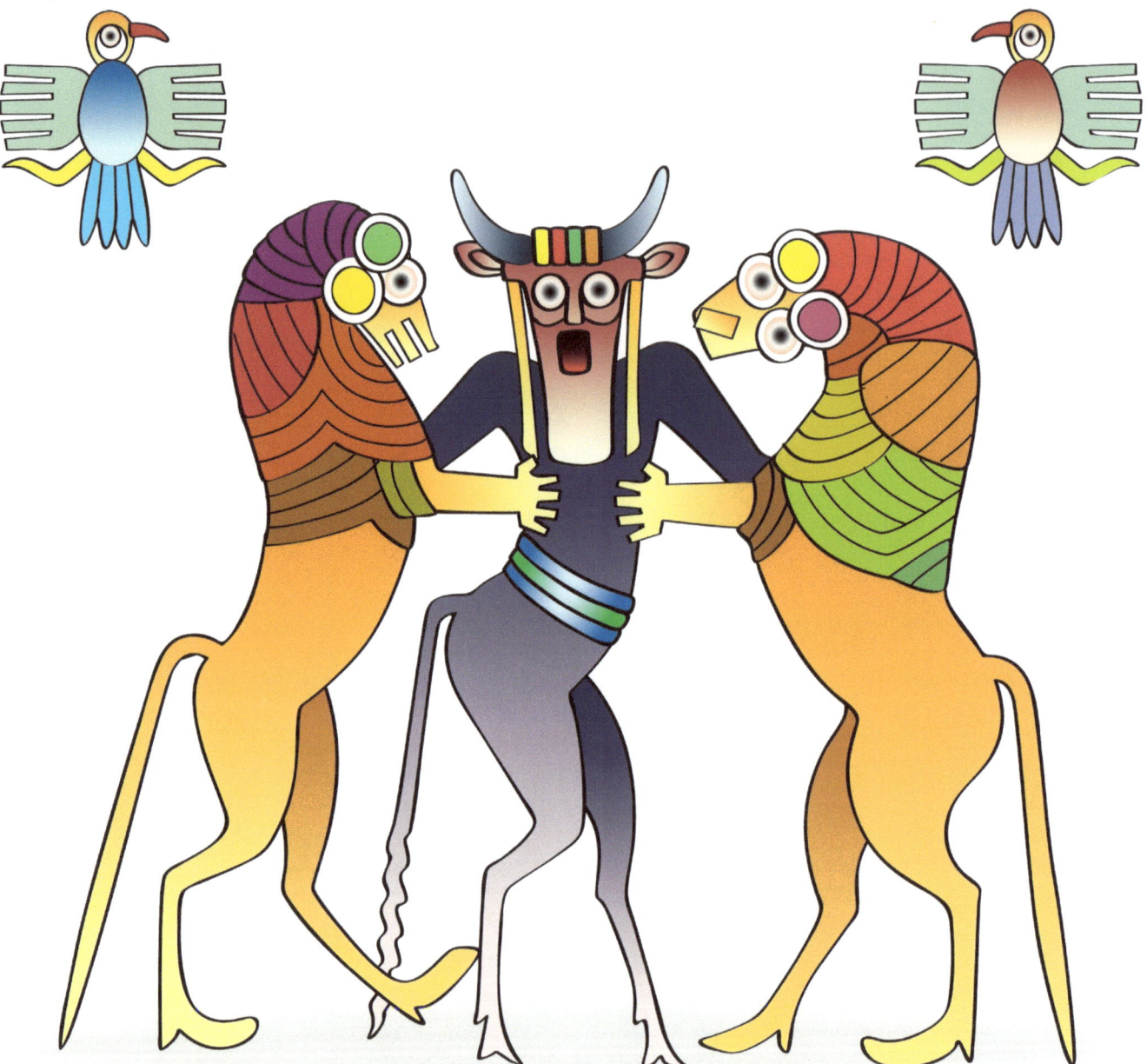

Early dynastic seal impression with animals and mythological creatures.
Between 2700 and 2370 B.C.E.

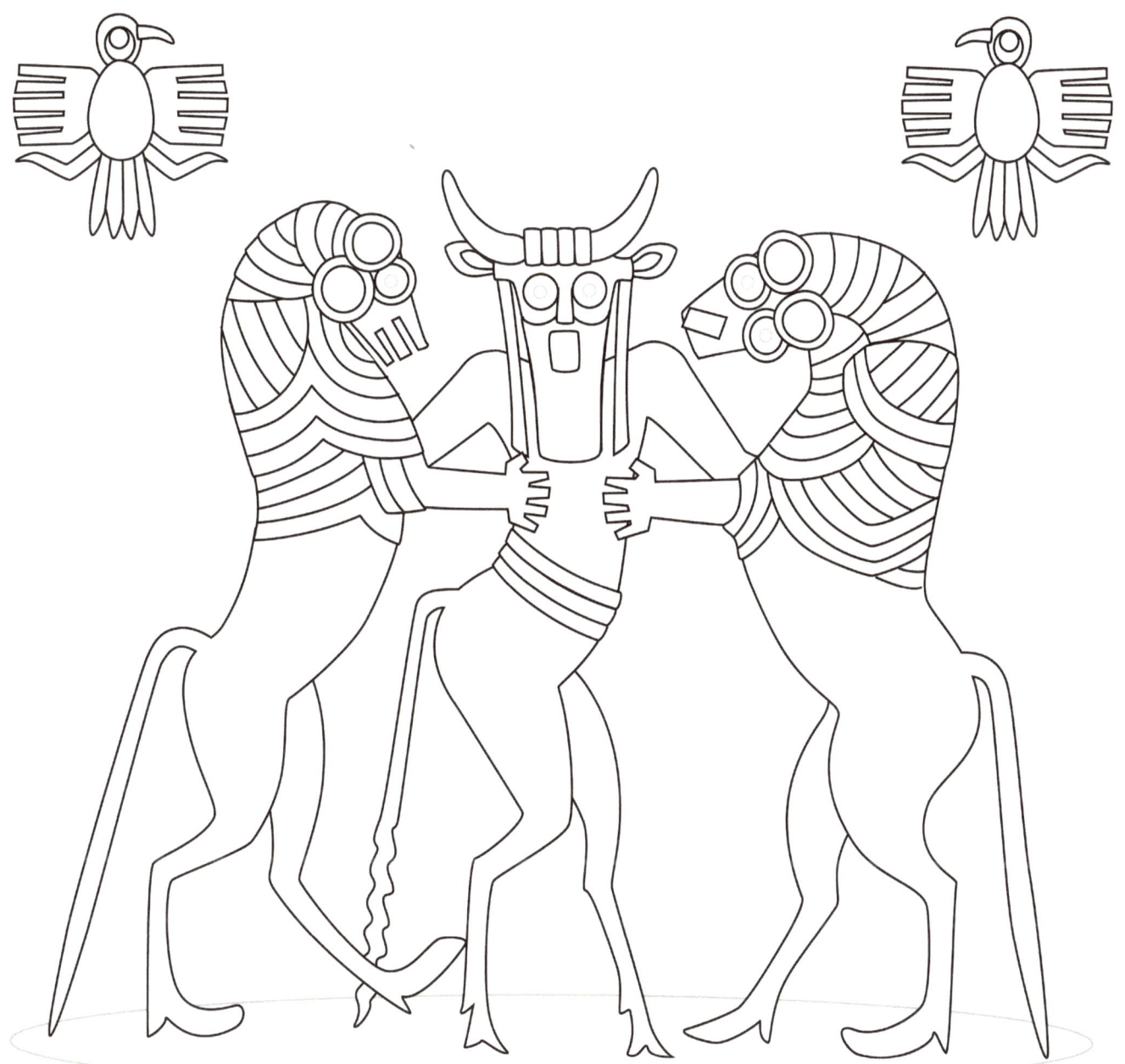

Color the drawings above using your preferred choice of colors.

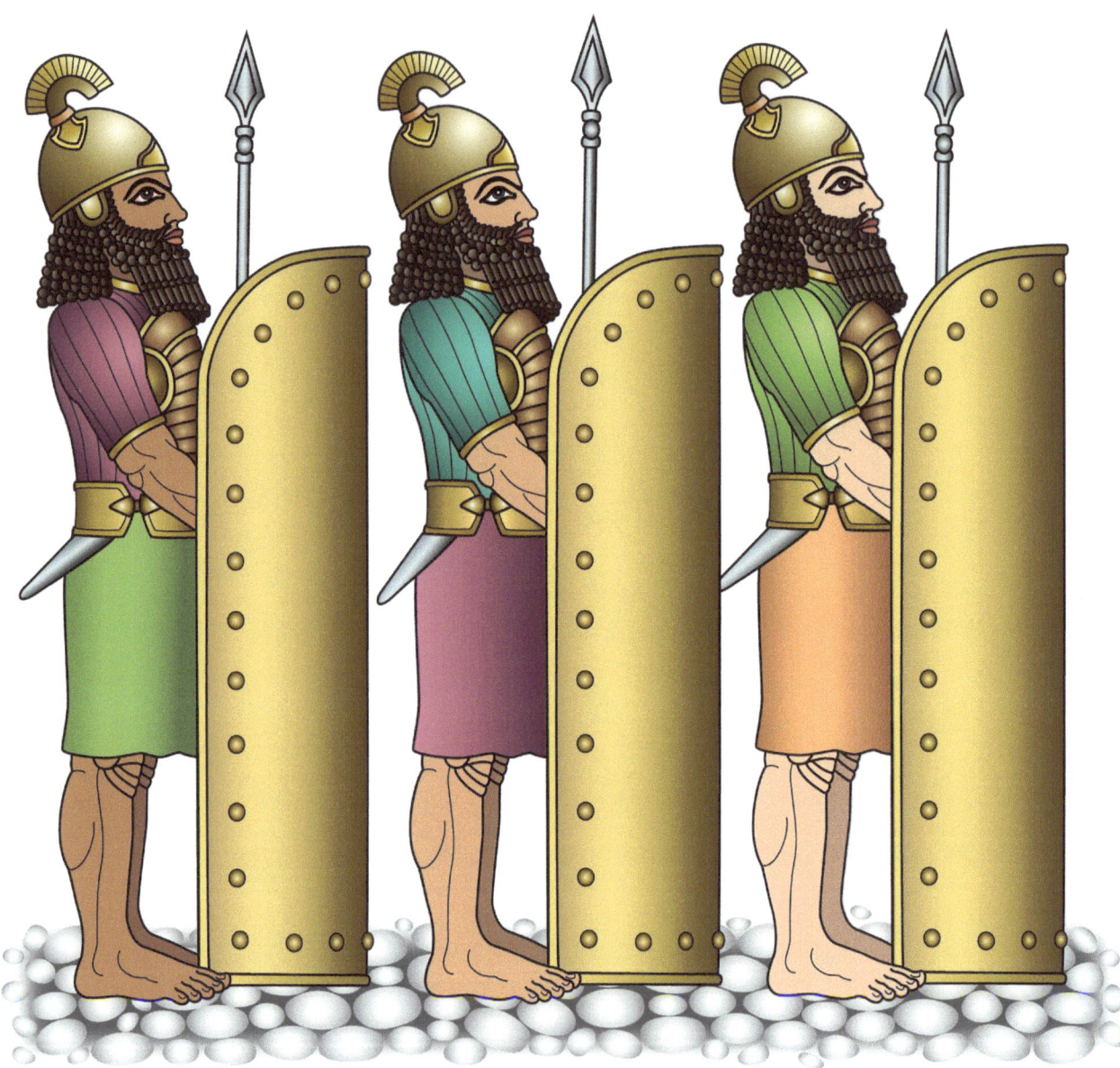

Assyrian King Ashurbanipal's soldiers (668 - 631 B.C.E.).

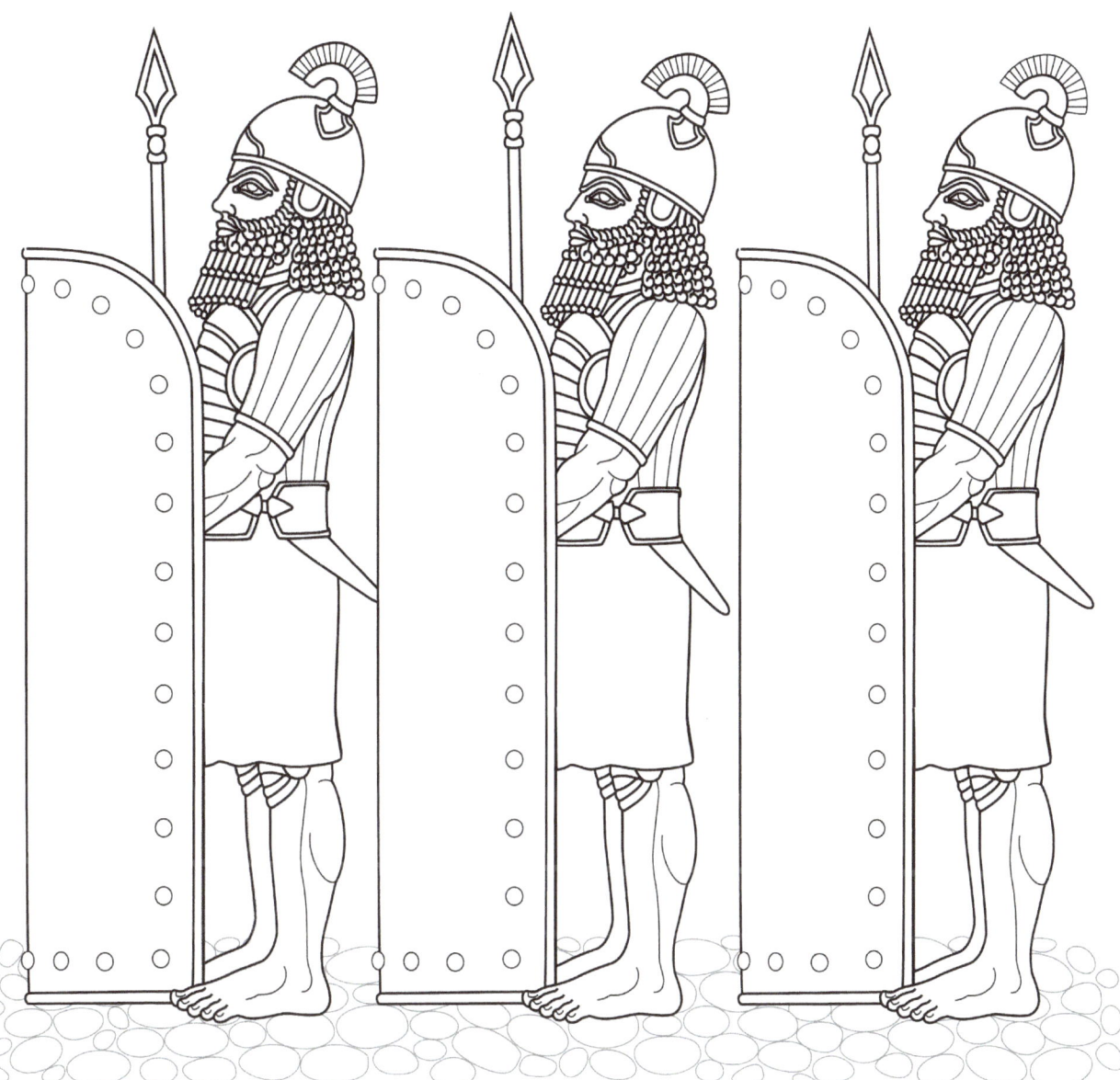

Color the drawings above using your preferred choice of colors.

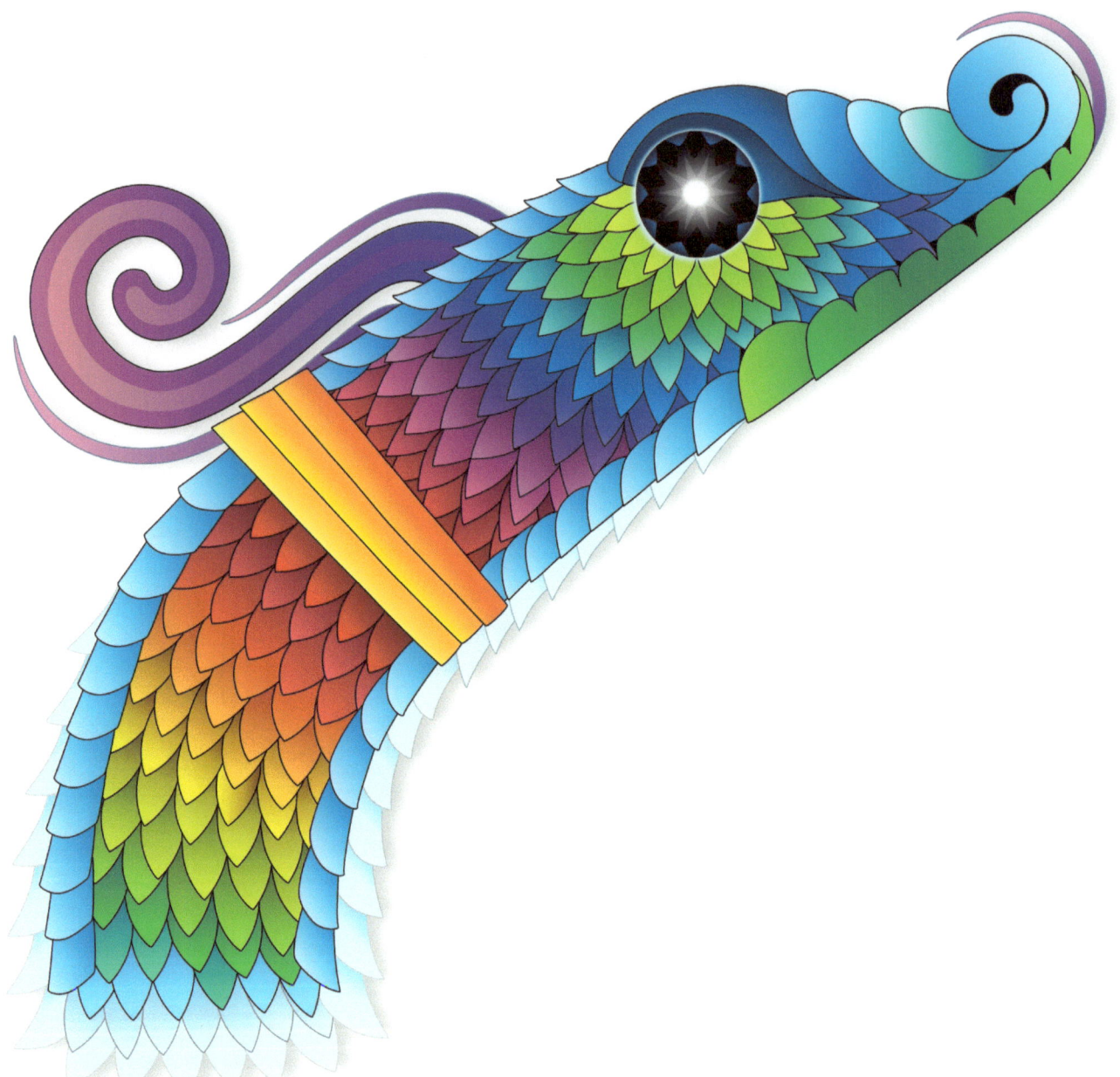

Relief of a dragon head created with glazed terracotta bricks during King Nebuchadnezzar-II reign, 605 - 562 B.C.E.

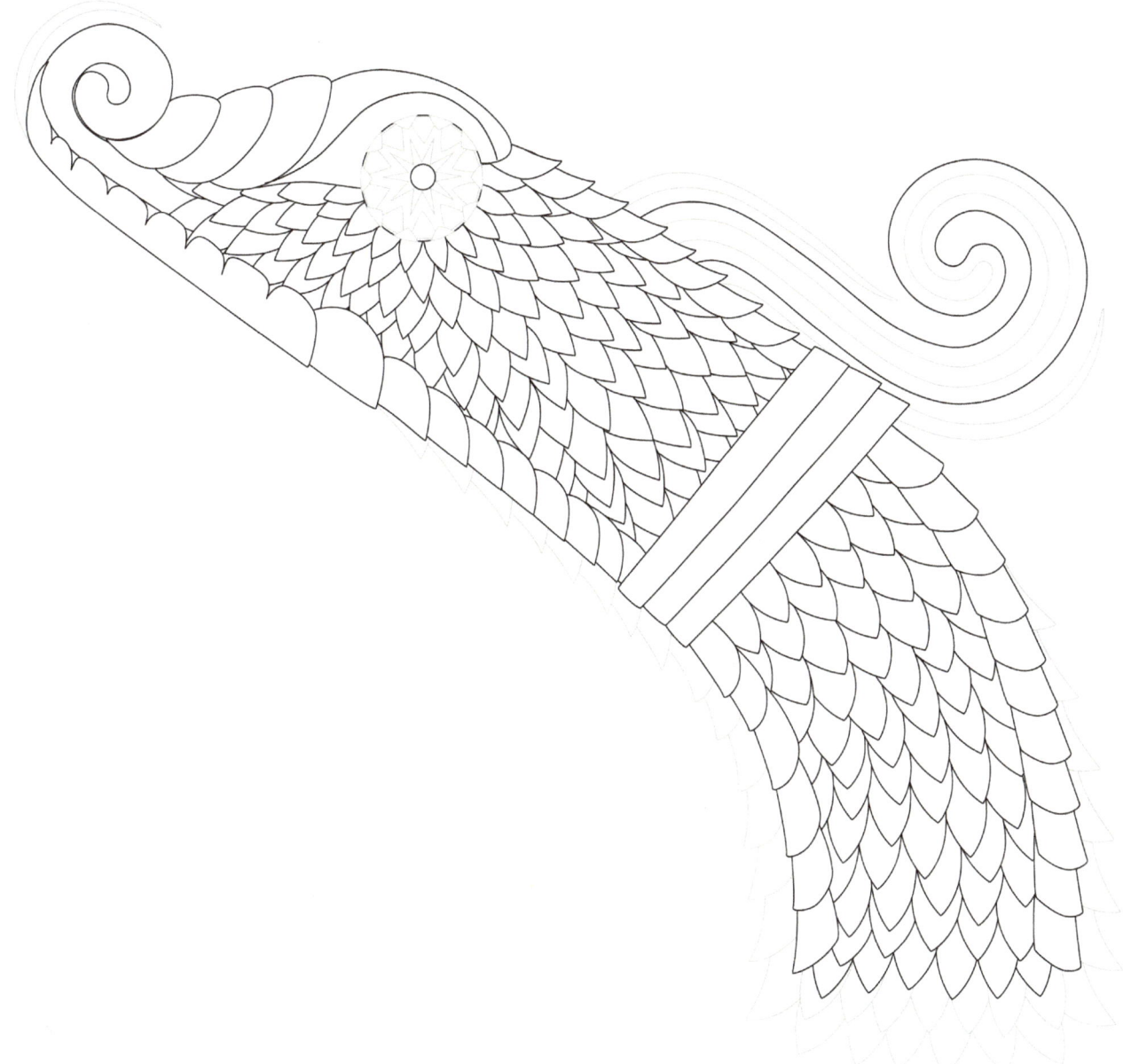

Color the drawing above using your preferred choice of colors.

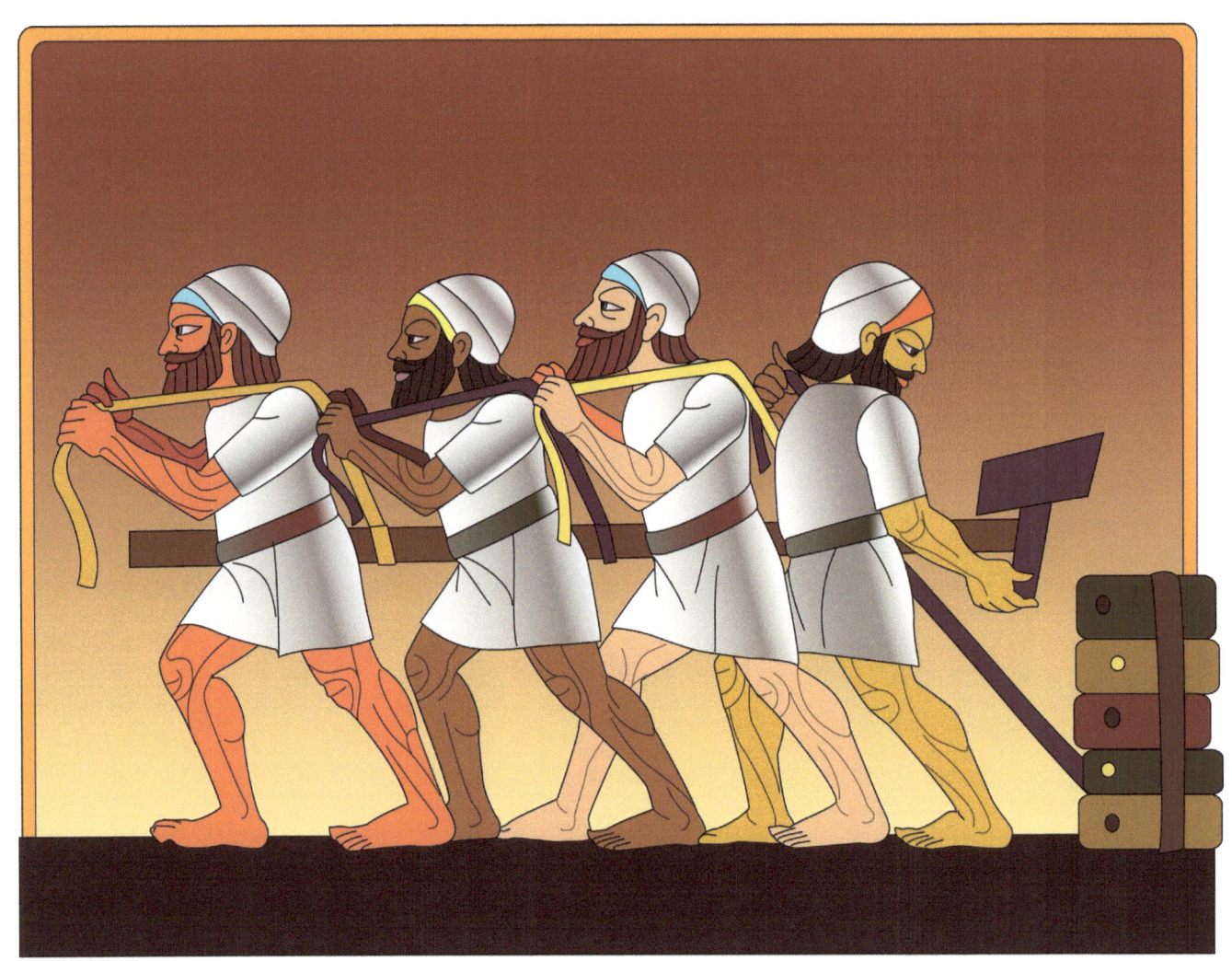

A relief work showing the deported populations hauling timber
to be used for roofing of Sargon's new capital at Khorsabad. Circa 6th Century B.C.E.

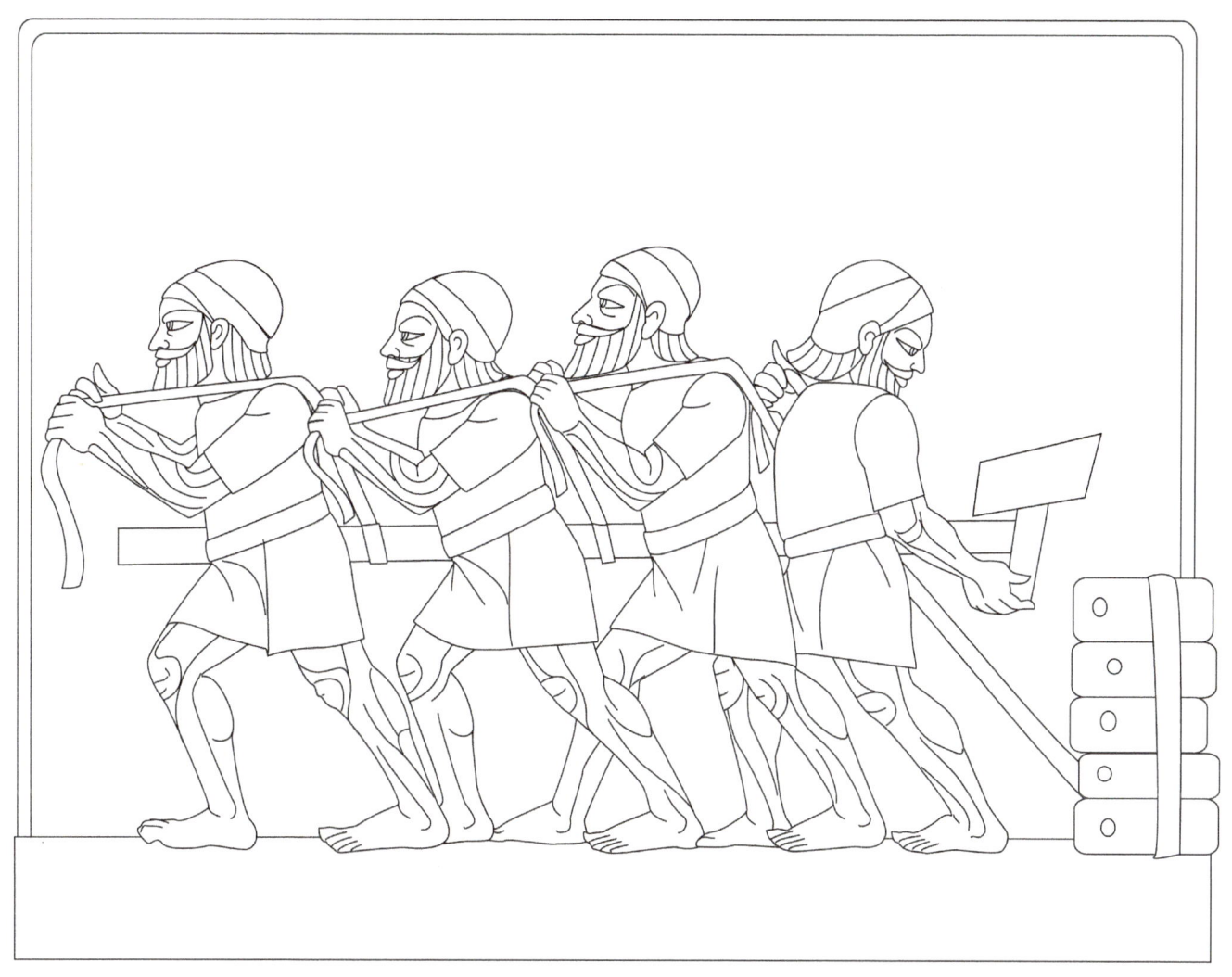

Color the drawing above using your preferred choice of colors.

Imdugud, the Lion-headed eagle of
Sumerian mythology with wings spread. 2600 - 2400 B.C.E.

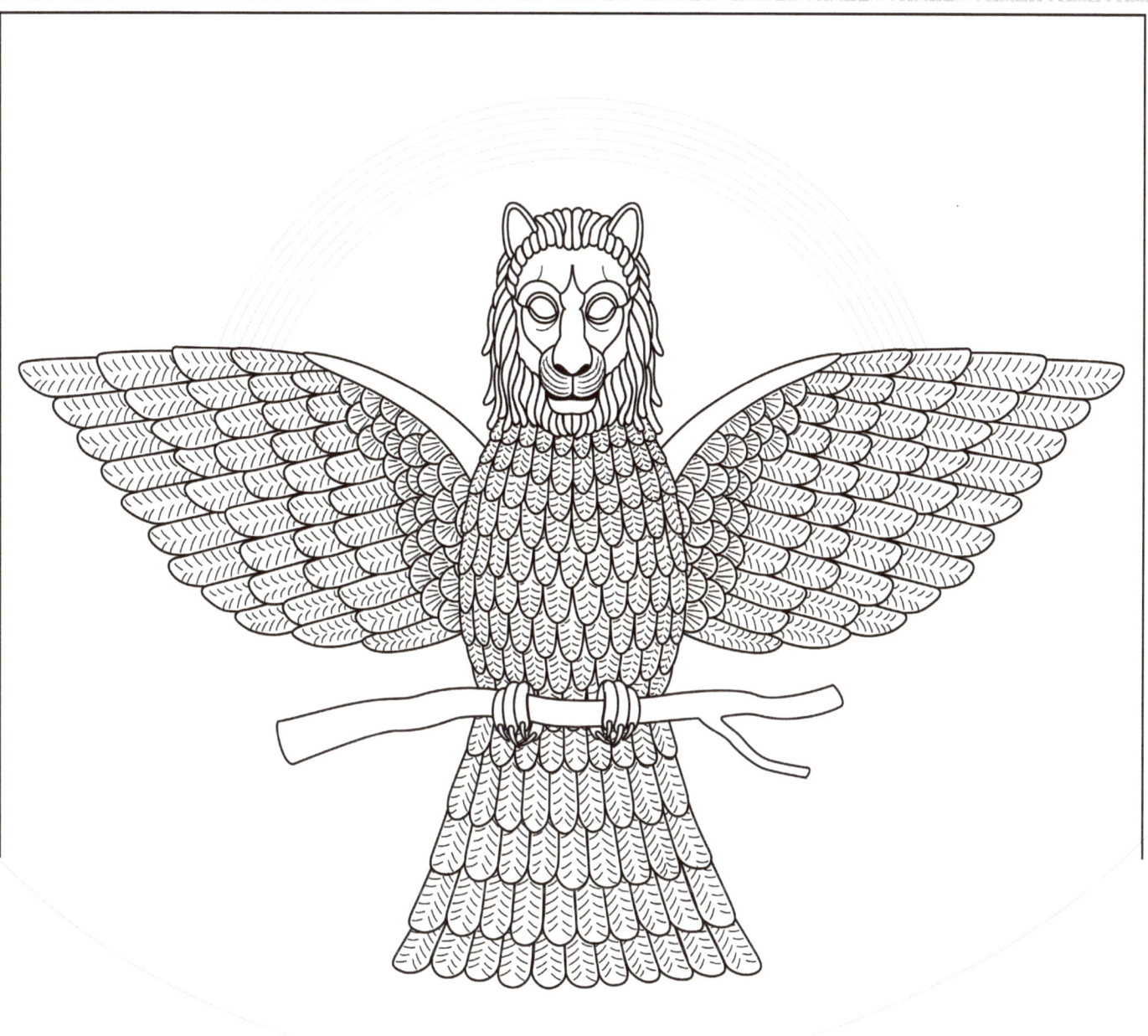

Color the drawing above using your preferred choice of colors.

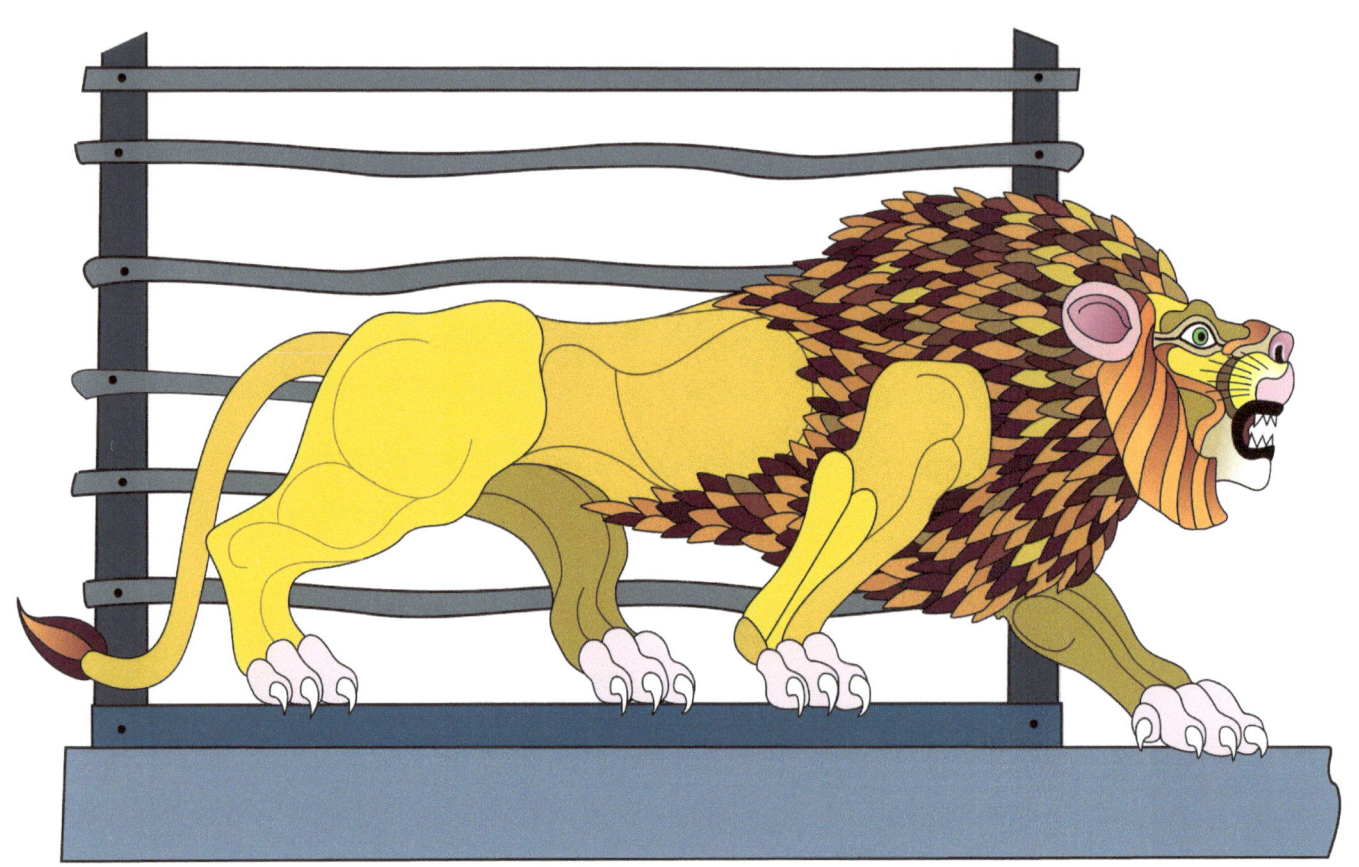

A Lion is released from its cage for King Ashurbanipal to hunt.
Lion was a royal beast and had to be conveyed to the king whenever possible. 7th Century B.C.E.

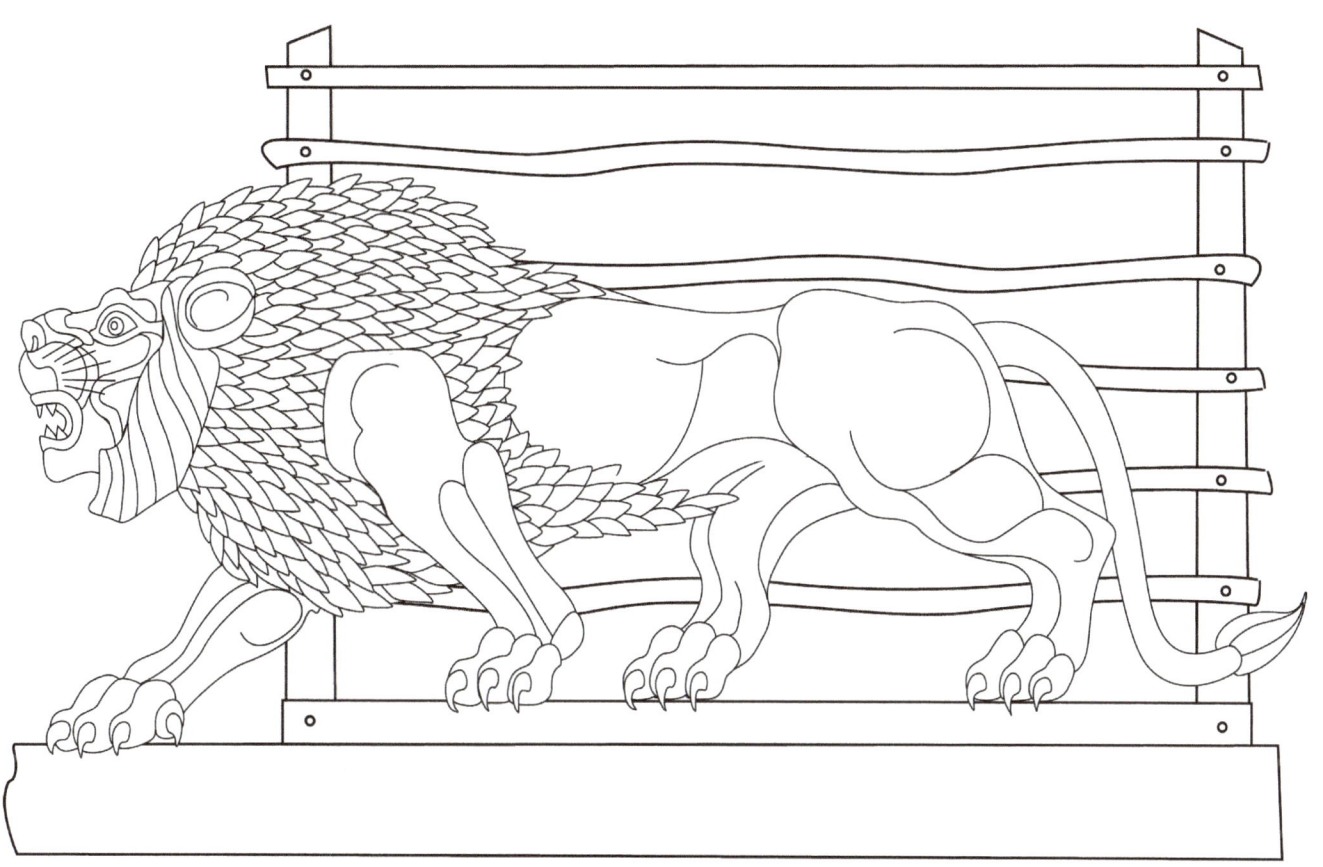

Color the drawing above using your preferred choice of colors.

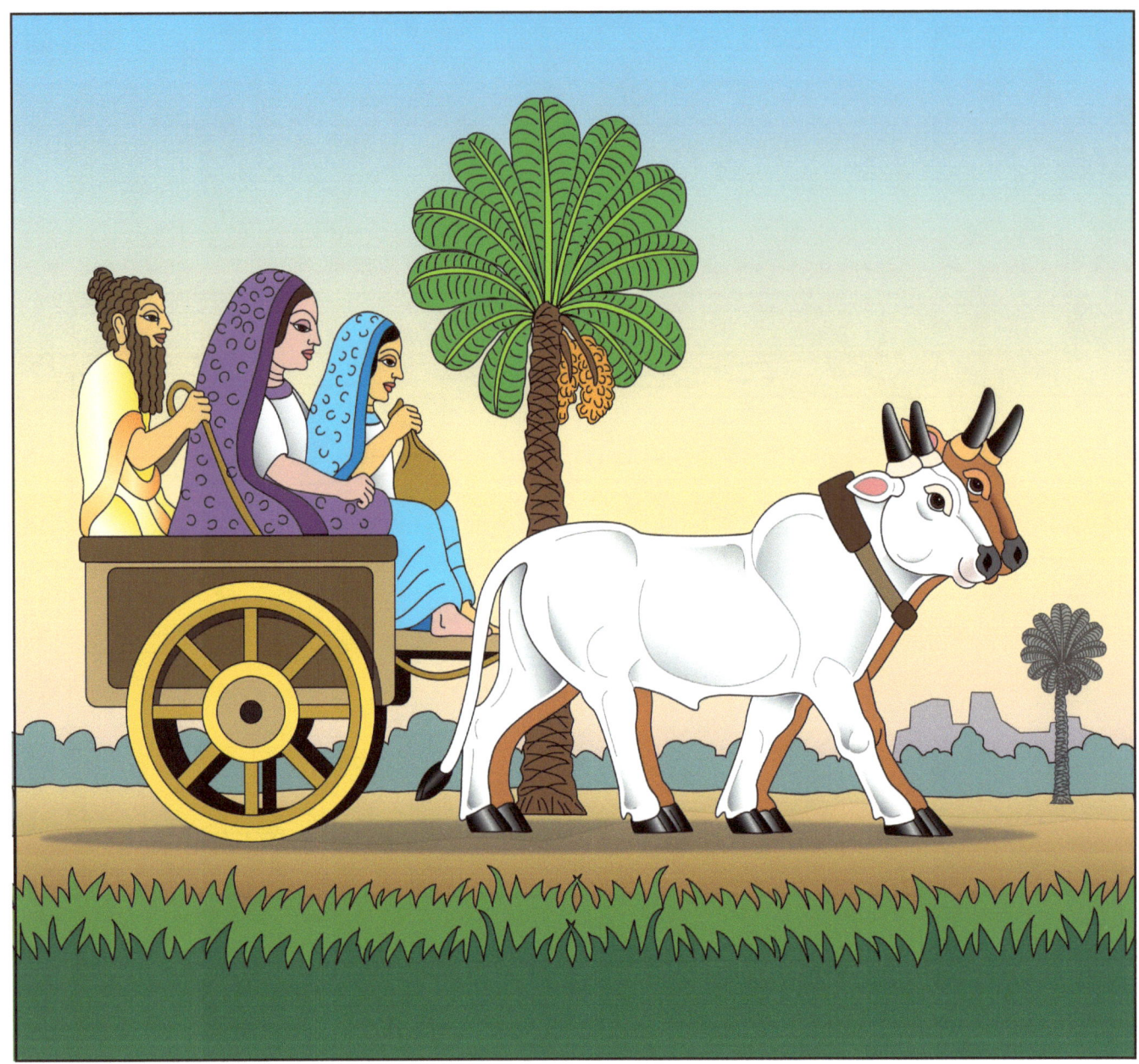

A relief on Tiglath-Pileser- III. Nimrud, 730 B.C.E.

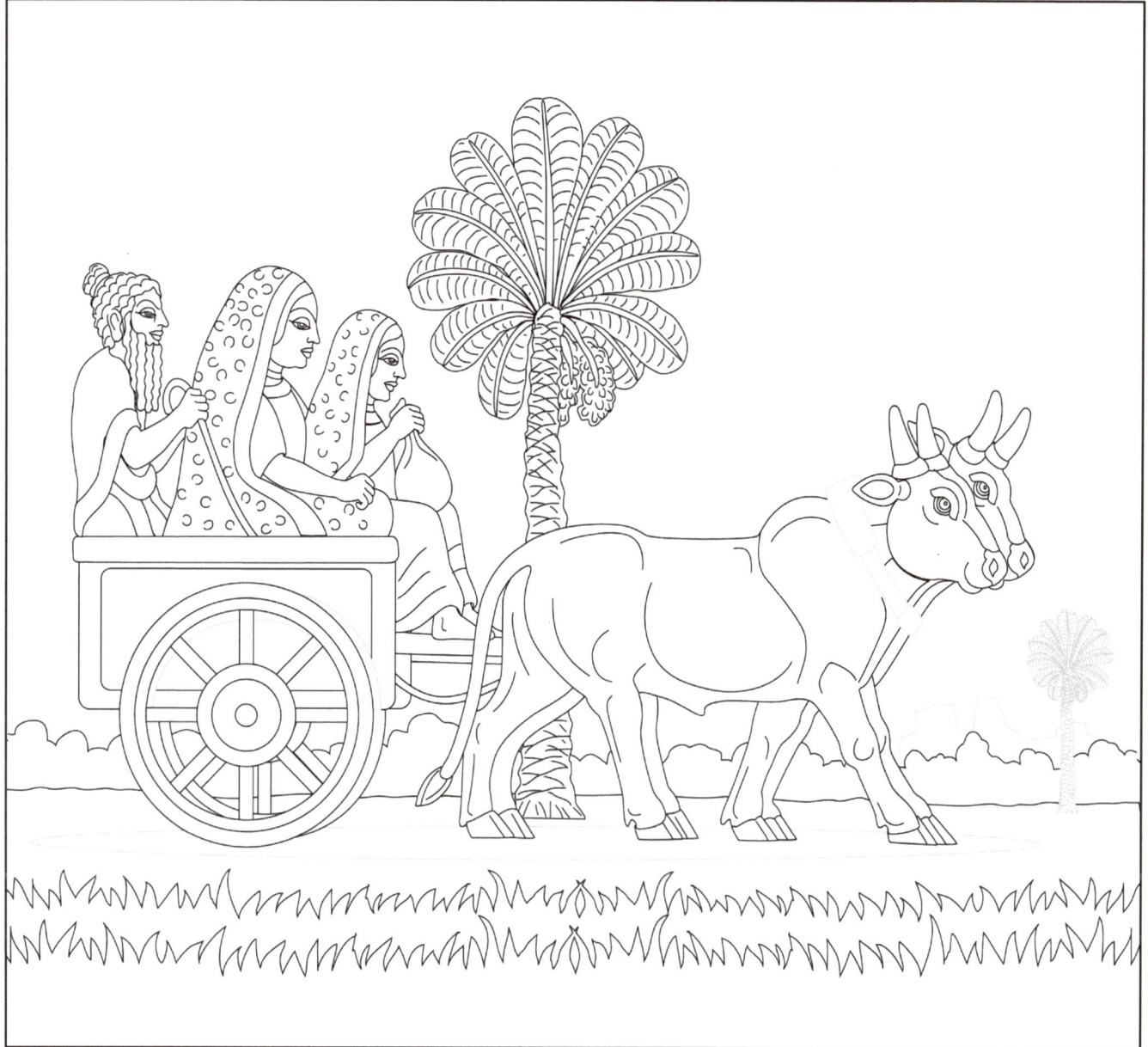

Color the drawing above using your preferred choice of colors.

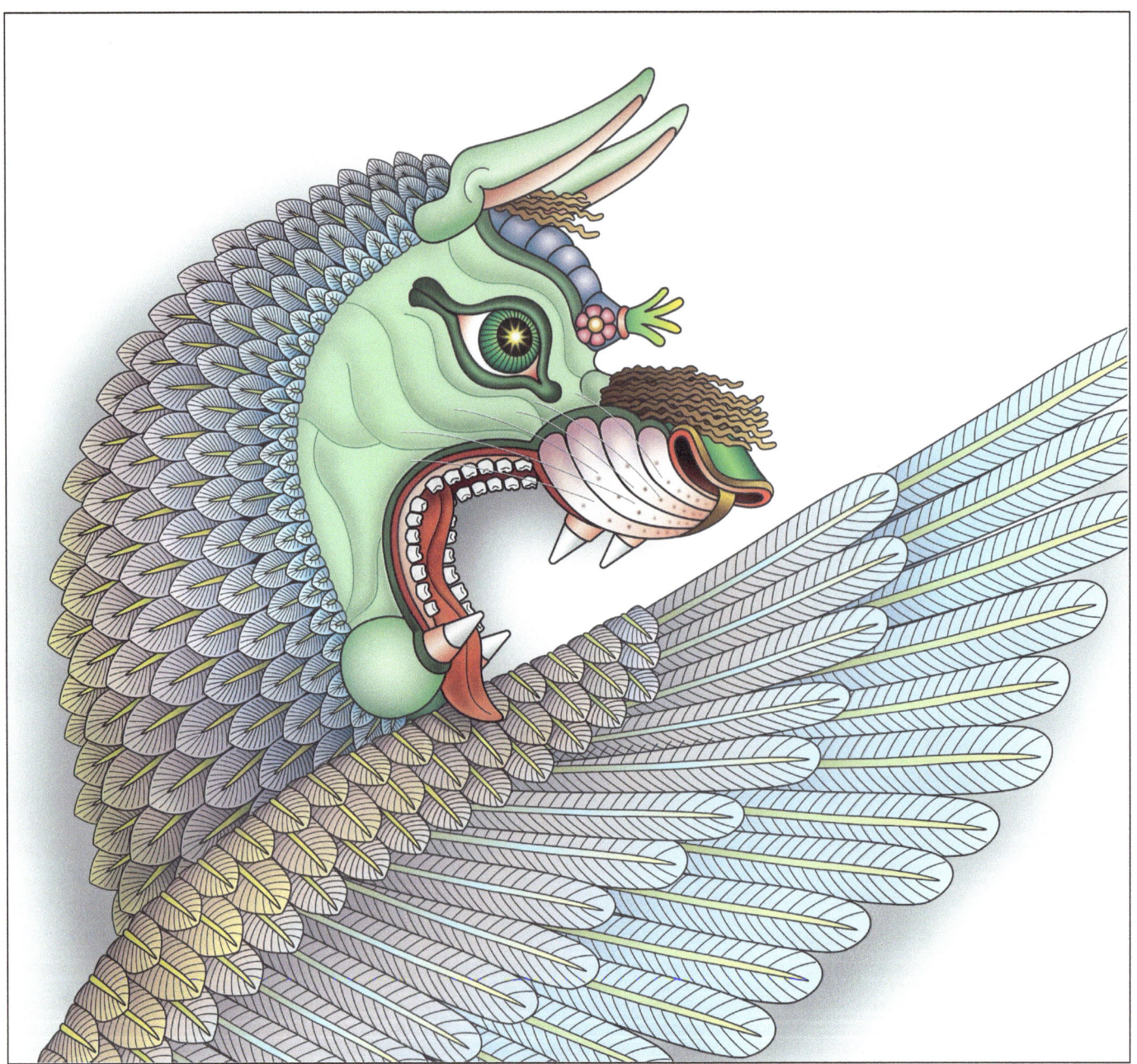

Winged Monster - a mythical character. Sculpted relief in one of Ashurbanipal rooms.

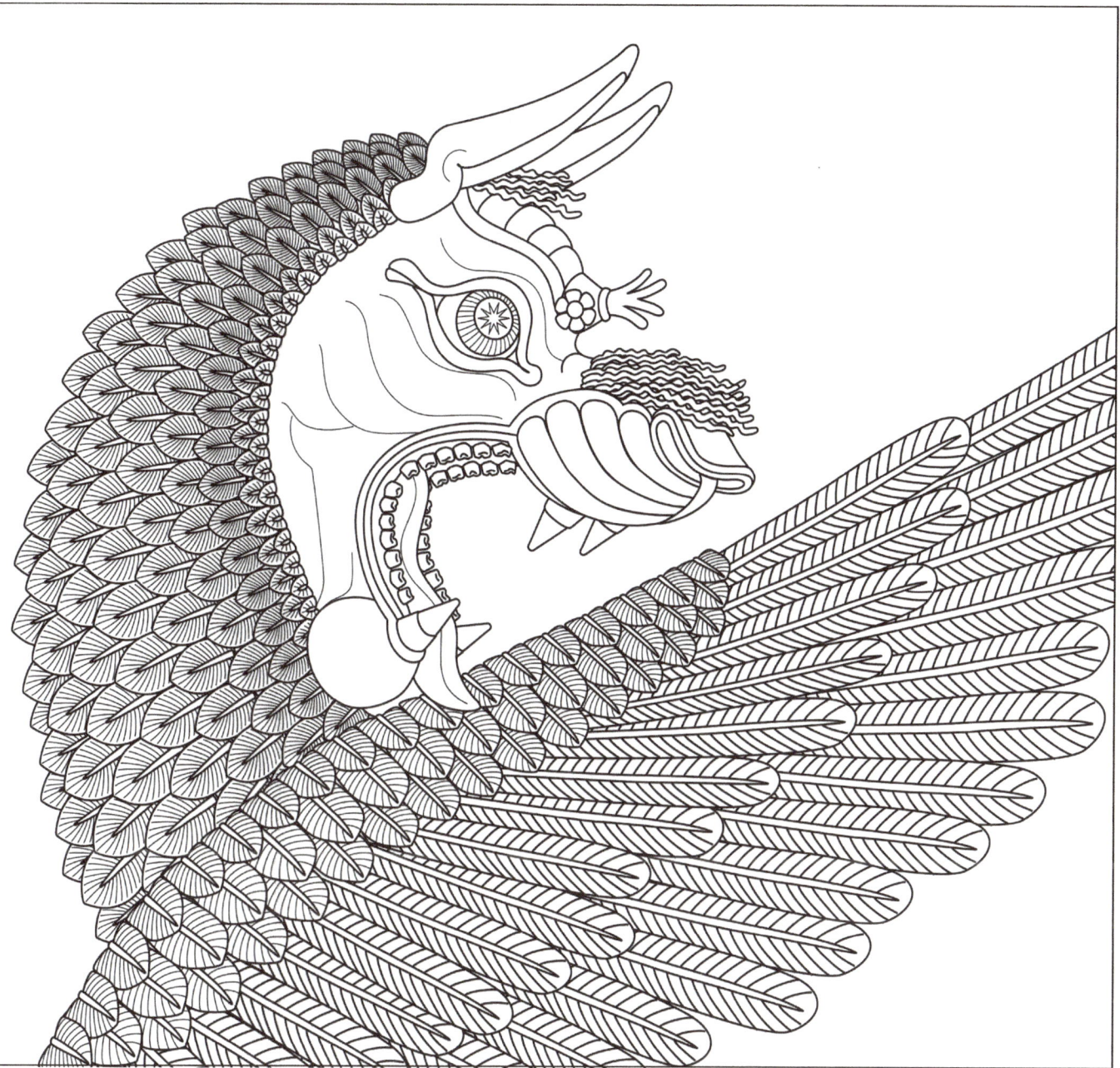

Color the drawing above using your preferred choice of colors.

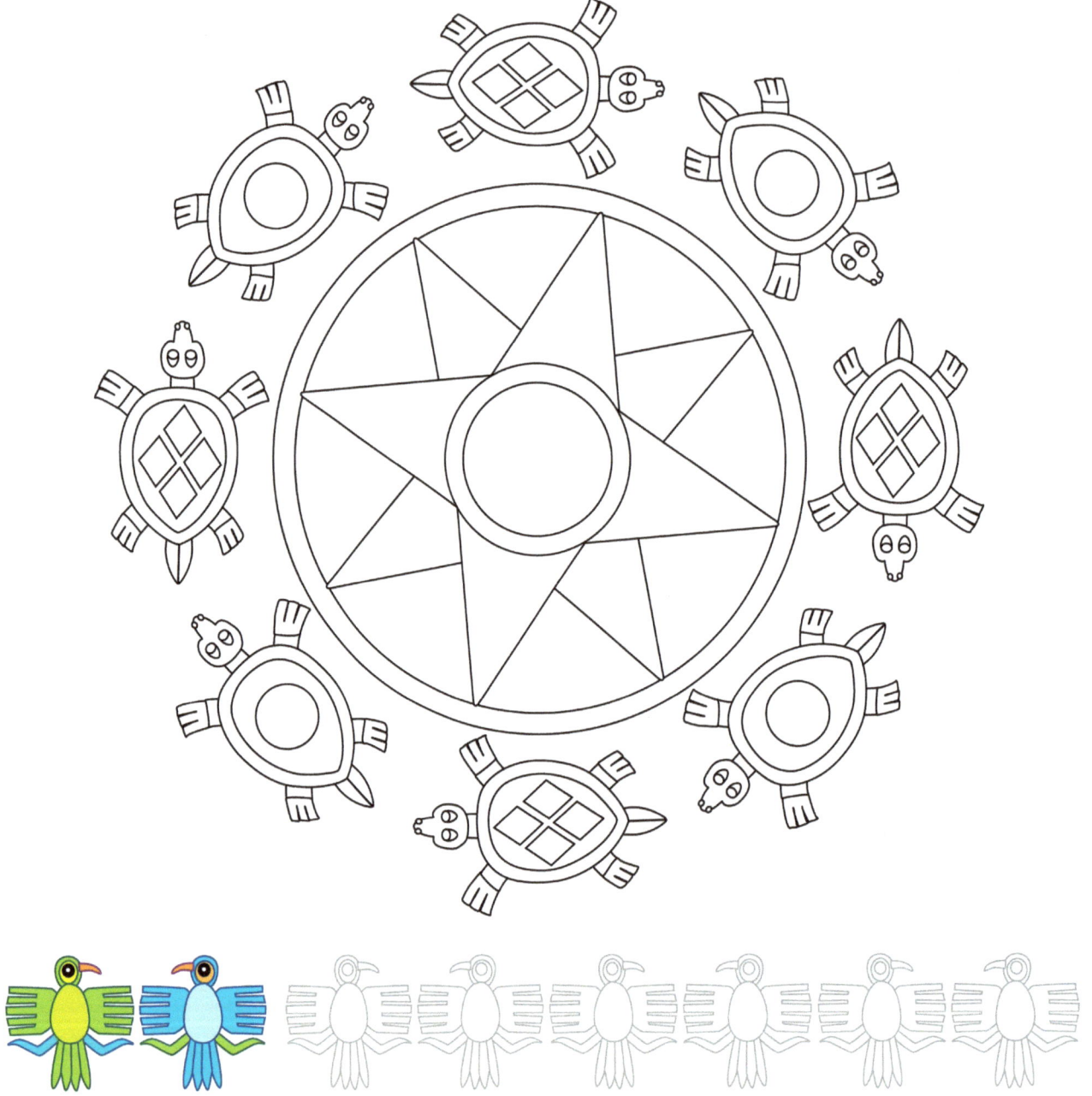

Using these images as examples, create your own piece using the elements found in Babylonian Art.

Babylonian Art

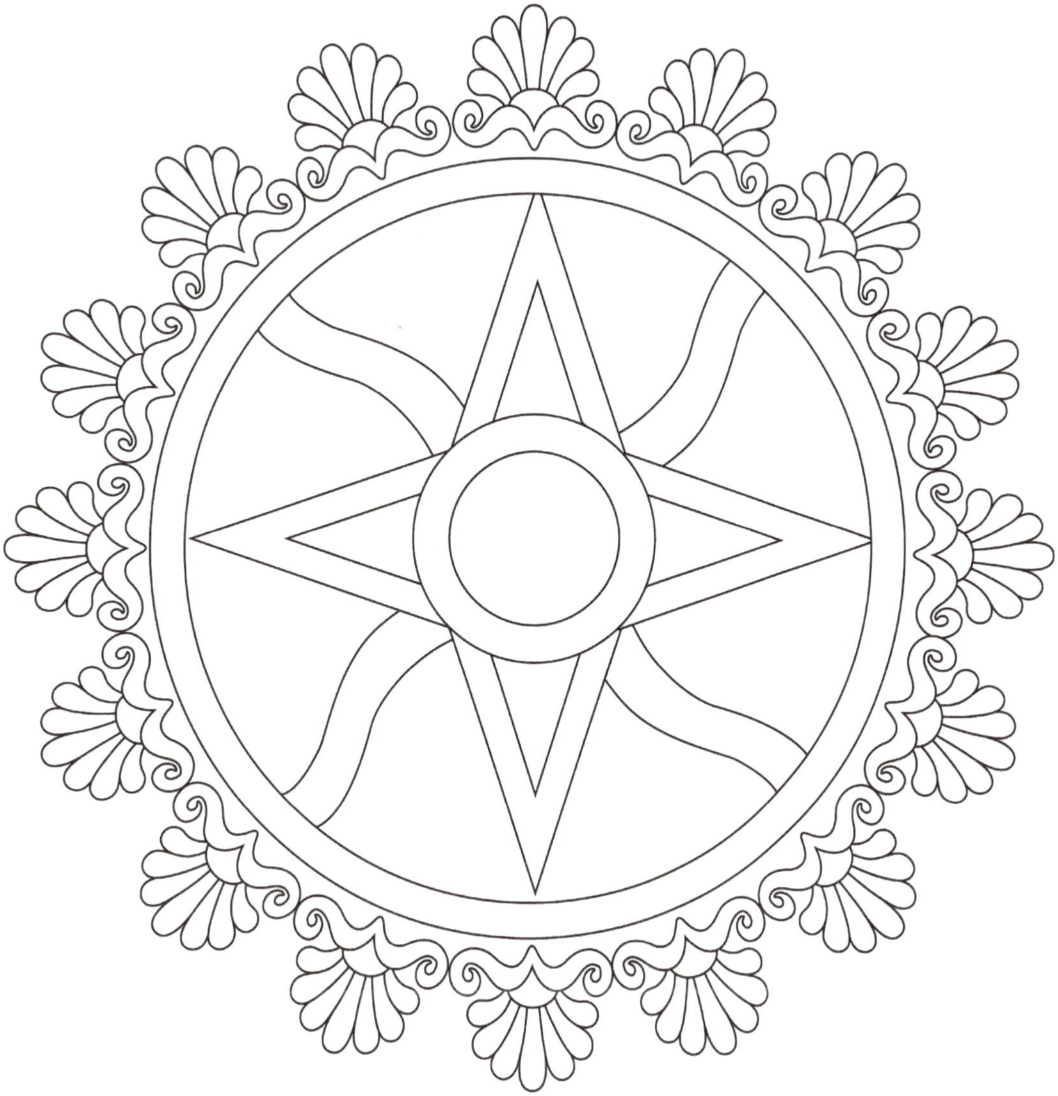

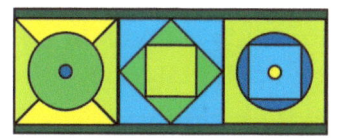

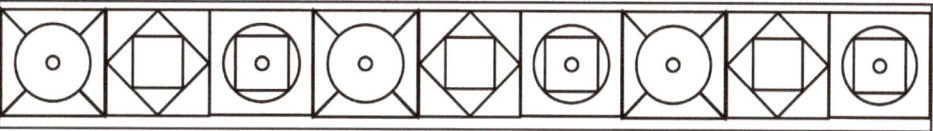

Color the drawings above using your preferred choice of colors.

= a synopsis of =
Babylonian Art

The earliest politico-religious and artistic expressions of man within a mature culture were found in the region known today as the ancient Middle East. The civilization stretches from Egypt and Anatolia in the West to the Iranian plateau in the East and beyond. The Babylonian Civilization was a natural offspring of the Sumerian Civilization. Babylon means "The Gate of Gods," and was the administrative capital when the Ur dominated the central and the southern Mesopotamian Civilization.

A double, four-sided wall five miles long, flanked by a canal used as a moat defended the city. The system of cuneiform writing on clay and seals originated there in 3100 B.C.E. This writing system was adopted in other neighboring countries.

Babylon became the spiritual and temporal capital of the region during the reign of King Hammurabi (1792 - 1750 B.C.E.). There are bas-relief sculptures showing King Hammurabi accepts the text of laws from the God Shamash, a patron of justice. King Hammurabi is also represented in sculptures, kneeling in prayer. The main gate was decorated with figures of dragons, the emblem of the God Marduk, and the bulls, associated with Adad, the God of storms with enameled bricks. Terracotta reliefs that were discovered are elegant and dates back to the early 2000 B.C.E. The terracotta sculptures and carpentry depicts the daily life of the Babylonians.

After King Hammurabi's death, Mesopotamia was torn for centuries by foreign invaders, who razed the city of Babylon. In 612 B.C.E., under the rule of King Nebuchadnezzar II, Babylonia developed to perfection creating the most striking artworks with their relief molded polychrome glazed brick walls. It contains up to 575 reliefs of lions, dragons, and bulls of all created with incredible craftsmanship.

In the king's palace, the Ishtar Gate, and the royal processional road, made Babylonia a city of splendor and unrivaled magnificence. Skilled artisans drew upon materials and styles from an area bounded by Egypt in the west all the way to India in the east. Unfortunately, the new splendor was short lived, as Babylonia fell with more invasions and eventually crumbled.

Other Titles In This Series

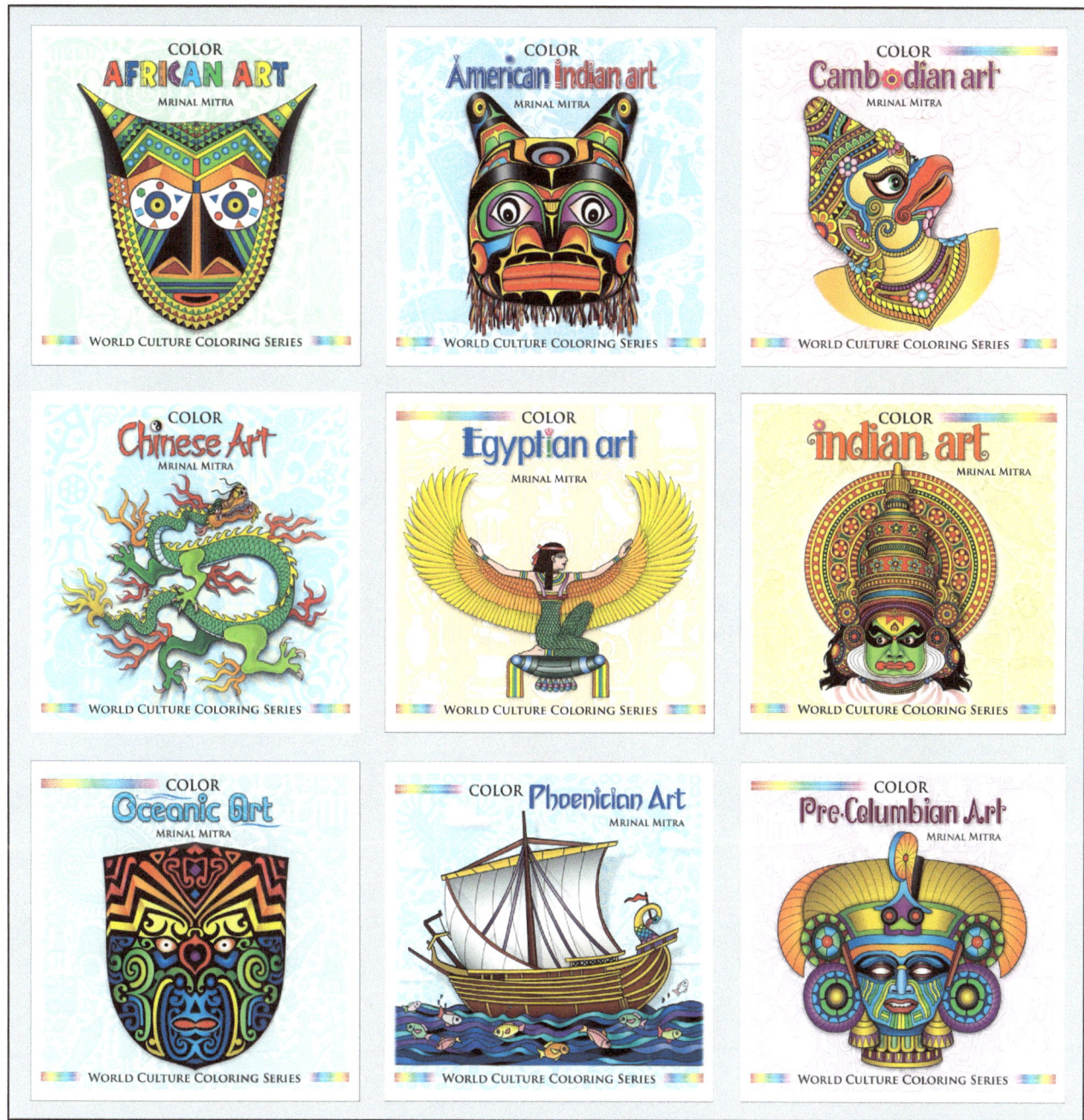

COLOR
AFRICAN ART
MRINAL MITRA
WORLD CULTURE COLORING SERIES

COLOR
American Indian art
MRINAL MITRA
WORLD CULTURE COLORING SERIES

COLOR
Cambodian art
MRINAL MITRA
WORLD CULTURE COLORING SERIES

COLOR
Chinese Art
MRINAL MITRA
WORLD CULTURE COLORING SERIES

COLOR
Egyptian art
MRINAL MITRA
WORLD CULTURE COLORING SERIES

COLOR
Indian art
MRINAL MITRA
WORLD CULTURE COLORING SERIES

COLOR
Oceanic Art
MRINAL MITRA
WORLD CULTURE COLORING SERIES

COLOR **Phoenician Art**
MRINAL MITRA
WORLD CULTURE COLORING SERIES

COLOR
Pre-Columbian Art
MRINAL MITRA
WORLD CULTURE COLORING SERIES

AVAILABLE FROM AMAZON.COM, CREATESPACE.COM, AND OTHER RETAIL OUTLETS

Acknowledgement

First and foremost, this series would not be possible without the number of great historical art found within the different cultural regions around the world.

In addition, we would like to acknowledge the variety of publishing's from all over the world for allowing us to learn about their fascinating ancestral art and culture. With this provided knowledge, we have hoped to have represented the art as splendidly as you have supplied it.

About the Author

Mrinal Mitra has earned a number of prestigious awards, both Indian and International, and received honors for his outstanding illustrations. Some of his recognitions include; The Noma Concours Award, Japan (twice), Illustrators Award, and Children's Choice Award, India, and honors from German Television "Transtel", BRNO- CSSR, TIBI- Iran, and UNICEF, New York.

Many of his talented artworks have been exhibited in several different countries such as; India, Japan, Italy, Czech Republic, Iran, and New Zealand. Mitra has authored, designed and illustrated trade and educational children's books for many Indian as well as Multinational Book Publishers around the globe.

Copyright: Mrinal Mitra, 2014

Printed by CreateSpace, An Amazon.com. Company
Available from Amazon.com, CreateSpace.com, and other retail outlets

For further inquiry please contact Mrinal Mitra at: mitra_mrinal@hotmail.com

www.ingramcontent.com/pod-product-compliance
Lightning Source LLC
Chambersburg PA
CBHW050840180526
45159CB00004B/1968